Windrush Forbears

Black People in Lambeth
1700 - 1900

Jon Newman

department for
education and skills

Lambeth
Archives

First published 2002 by Lambeth Archives
Minet Library, 52 Knatchbull Rd. London SE5 9QY

ISBN No. 0-9543173-0-0.

British Library Cataloguing-in Publication Data
a catalogue record for this book is available from the British Library

Design by London Borough of Lambeth, Communication Centre
Printed and bound by Jewell Printers Ltd

Contents

Plates

All plates are between pages 62 and 63

Foreword: Making History

We are becoming accustomed to discussing what history is, and how it is made. Rather than assuming that archivists and historians are preserving and recounting the past objectively we are much more ready to question, less prepared to leave these processes to professionals. Many now recognise that history is mediated and interpreted, and thus involves subjective judgements about what is significant and should be included, and what is insignificant and should be excluded: it is not simply being a collection of self-evidently true events, or a neutral record of the past. This awareness has been central to the development of the body of work about black history in Britain.

The opening up of debates about history, memorialising, objectivity, and the notion of heritage is not an entirely recent activity – historians of the working classes and of women have been arguing for a more inclusive notion of what constitutes historical significance for decades. But now the debates have gained more urgency for those people descended from African, Caribbean and Asian migrants who see the way that the black presence has been all but expunged from conventional British historical narratives, and the negative impact this has on both black and white communities.

How have these arguments impacted on what historians and archivists do and how they do it? The question of historical exclusivity is seen as an unwelcome intruder into matters of professional custom and practice for some. In many respects, archives have been the most difficult of areas to penetrate with regard to such issues. Although there has been a surge of interest in tracing family histories through local archives and the internet, most members of the public would not be able to say for certain if there was an archive in their neighbourhood, let alone where it was and what it had to offer. In addition many archivists are really at the beginning of the journey that moves them from providing specialist facilities for the initiated to promoting accessible archive use to the general public. Shrouded in the mysteries of ritualistic use of cotton gloves and lead pencils, and the scientific rigours of strictly controlled temperatures and specialist cleaning regimes, it is little wonder that so many people have no idea how to use an archive or of what benefit it might be to them.

Black History Month, in October each year since 1987, has done much to raise awareness about the history of black diaspora peoples in Britain but one month in the year should not be the only instrument harnessed for this effort. There should be local, regional and national strategies for thinking about the role and potential of history and heritage in 21st century, culturally diverse Britain. London is clearly an important nodal point with its imperial past manifested in its wealth of heritage monuments and institutions, and its international links. The strength of London's position as a world city is based on its position as a key centre for global financial transactions and services but is also dependent on the breadth and heritage of its cultural institutions, and its reputation as one of the most cosmopolitan cities in the world. Also crucial in this respect is its reputation for producing talented, leading edge cultural entrepreneurs many of whom are from the African and Asian diasporas, or whose work is strongly influenced by these sources. London did not become like this overnight of course, but where is it possible to trace how it has reached that point? In very few places in London are these connections made in any kind of meaningful historical sense.

The possibilities raised by the traces of the black presence revealed in Lambeth archives are suggestive. What if this exercise was to be carried out elsewhere? Let's say that the relevant funding and strategic agencies came together and decided that extending this research project would make a major, lasting contribution to understanding the flow of black and Asian peoples into, out of and across London. Such a project could be organised in a way that was not too costly and would embed this type of work as a part of the 'normal' work of an archive. It would raise the profile of the valuable human and material assets of archives amongst black and other communities significantly. As more peoples come to live and work here from parts of the world that were not subject to British colonial rule, the demands for the articulation of these histories will gain momentum: it is an issue that is not going to disappear.

The popular perception of black people arriving here for the first time in 1948 on the Windrush was already beginning to be shattered by the time of the publication of Peter Fryer's *Staying Power*, and by the academic researches of the mid 1980s. Evidence was revealed of the presence of African peoples in Britain since at least Roman times; more work has been published, producing a complex, rich but uneven narrative. There are still gaps and many questions to be asked but there is a sense that the gains made in arguing for a more nuanced sense of British history will continue to build. The publication of Lambeth Archives research findings represents a valuable contribution to the project of making visible the historical presence of black people in Britain.

Lola Young
Head of Culture, Greater London Authority

Introduction

This book is the outcome of a two year project to research the documentary evidence of Lambeth's earliest black and Asian communities. The initial idea was triggered by the 1998 Windrush anniversary celebrations. At that time, when the significance and diversity of the post-war Caribbean migration to Britain was being celebrated across the country and was achieving national coverage on television and in the press, one could almost sense a new historical myth being formed; the notion that there had been no black people in England before 1948. The London borough of Lambeth had very strong links with the Windrush voyagers. With Brixton a recognised centre for subsequent migration from the Caribbean and West Africa in the 1950s and 1960s, it was important to question this easy assumption. To counter this and to move on from our own work celebrating the events of 1948, Lambeth Archives developed a detailed project to attempt to discover and recover the documentation of longer established black and Asian communities in South London.

We already had evidence of Lambeth links with Africa, India and the Caribbean. Wealthy merchants whose money derived from slave-worked sugar plantations or from investments in the East India Company were living in Streatham and Clapham in the eighteenth century; and wills and other title deeds document their involvement in slavery.[1] Other men like Noble Jones, born in Lambeth in 1702, emigrated to the New World to help manage the slave economy. Jones worked as a surveyor, mapping the recently acquired British colony of Georgia; his son Wymberley Jones purchased a 450-acre plantation and slaves there in 1750 and named it "Lambeth".[2] At the end of the nineteenth century the sugar baron Henry Tate, the head of the family firm that was to become Tate and Lyle and whose Liverpool and London sugar businesses relied first on slave and then on free plantation labour in the Caribbean, was living at his mansion, Park Hill, in Streatham.

The abolitionist movement of the late eighteenth and early nineteenth century also had local champions. The activities of the Clapham sect, a group of wealthy evangelical Christians living in that area, were well documented. The MP William Wilberforce, who

---

[1] For example William Vassall of Clapham Common lived on slave plantation income from his lands in Hanover parish, Jamaica, [*CAS Occasional sheet, no.294*]. John Hankey of Streatham Common derived his wealth from sugar plantations and negro slaves in Grenada, which were left to his son in his will of 1773 (Pl. 7) [*LAD IV/35/32/10*]
[2] *Southwark and Lambeth Archaeological Society Newsletter* no. 90, June 2002

was the figurehead for the national campaign to abolish first the slave trade in 1807 and then slavery itself in 1833, lived on Clapham Common. So too did Henry Thornton, John Venn, the rector of Clapham and Zachary Macaulay who were all involved in very practical experiments in the anti-slavery movement including   the colony for freed slaves in Sierra Leone in the 1780s and the "African Academy" set up to educate Africans and freed slaves at Macaulay's house in Clapham.

There was no shortage of information about the local white establishment's involvement with Africa, Asia and the Caribbean in either benign or negative ways; but it was less clear whether there would be any real evidence of black or Asian people living in the area. The occasional discovery of the baptism or burial of a black person, often a servant or slave to a white master, in the parish registers suggested there might be more beneath the surface. If there were black people living in Lambeth then where else might they show up within the archives?

We knew that we were looking for a marginalised group of people most of whom would not have been literate. Information already available about black people in central London in the eighteenth and early nineteenth centuries suggested they were mainly servants, poor labourers and escaped slaves; in the words of one dismissive contemporary, "those who are not in livery are in rags".[3] These factors meant that many sources traditionally used by family historians were not going to be very relevant. Title deeds, leases, voters lists and local directories documented the fixed possessions and entitlements of the educated, property owning middle classes in Lambeth but they were all unlikely to register the existence of a transient underclass, be it black or white. And where there were significant exceptions, then the ethnicity of the person would be unlikely to be revealed by these records. The national census on the other hand was a very inclusive record series that would list everyone living in Lambeth. This was available from 1841 and after 1851 also included the place or country of birth of all people. This might have been a way of identifying first generation immigrants, but because it did not then give any information about a person's ethnicity (as it does now) there would be no way of knowing the race of a person born in, say, the West Indies or Africa except from the evidence of their name. For this reason we excluded it as an effective source

---

[3] James Tobin, 1785

The records searched needed to be continuous series that were inclusive and would also give information about race or ethnicity. We identified the local parish registers of baptisms, marriages and burials and the various "poor law" records that documented the assistance given to poor people in the parish as two possible record series. Local newspapers were only a phenomenon of the second half of the nineteenth century. Although they were not available for the earlier period of the project, we knew that these would be a good source of information for the period after 1850. Finally, because of Lambeth's unusual London-wide reputation as a place of entertainment in the late eighteenth and nineteenth centuries, we decided to look at the records of local theatres and pleasure gardens for evidence of black and Asian performers who might have appeared there.

Having obtained funding from the DfES, an 18-month research post was created to look in detail at the records at Lambeth Archives and other London record offices that might contain references to black and Asian people in Lambeth. The covering dates of the project were to be 1700 - 1900. This publication is now the outcome of that research. The findings have been organised as four chapters for the different classes of records searched. Each chapter contains an introduction that discusses the records, their limitations and the evidence they have produced; there are transcripts of all entries that refer to black or Asian people and illustrations from some of the original documents. Although the chapter introductions provide some local context and analysis of the results this is not intended to be a narrative about Lambeth's earlier black and Asian history. Rather it is a preliminary guide to the sources on the subject held by Lambeth Archives and other record offices and an exploration of the potential of some classes of records for use in further work on black history. We recognise that the work is by no means complete. The constraints of project funding meant that there was never going to be time to search, for example, all the poor law settlement examinations or all the local newspapers in the nineteenth century. Similarly the work done on theatre playbills is incomplete in the sense that we have only been able to look at the partial collections held by Lambeth Archives; there is clearly much more to be researched at national collections like the Theatre Museum in London and the Old Vic archive at Bristol.

We always knew that the local black and Asian community would be comparatively small. Lambeth's remote location and relatively sparse population in the eighteenth century compared with London-proper meant that the black presence was never going to match that of areas like Westminster or Tower Hamlets. But we also knew that it was important to the present day inhabitants of the borough that this information should be accessible. The findings are numerically modest but they are nevertheless compelling. It is clear that the white inhabitants of Lambeth would have been very aware of black people. By the end of the eighteenth century they had become a significant and visible minority who would have been regularly encountered as servants and working people; in the nineteenth century they were also familiar as performers at the local pleasure gardens, theatres and music halls and as the subject matter of much local journalism.

We hope that this book will be used to encourage and support further research. Although the project necessarily set itself quite limited parameters – the findings relate just to the London Borough of Lambeth and to the period before 1900 - we believe the project can stand as a model for other localities and communities in the way it takes the tools and techniques of the local historian and the family historian and applies them to black history. Much previous work in this area has used a biographical approach to celebrate achievement. Mary Seacole, Ira Aldridge and Master Juba all feature here in passing but their existing celebrity makes these additional findings the icing on an already baked cake. It is the recovery of so many unknown, and in some cases literally anonymous, black people, revealed for the first time through the records of their rites of passage, their material want or their passing local notoriety, that is the strength of this book; and one which provides the larger context for the achievements of the previously "known" black people in Lambeth.

We have simultaneously produced *Lambeth Black History Packs for Schools* for KS2 and KS4 pupils using materials from the project. These have been distributed to Lambeth schools and copies are also available from Lambeth Archives.

Jon Newman
Lambeth Archives

Acknowledgements

For a project that had its inception in 1998 and did not come to fruition until 2002 we have accumulated a lot of assistance and owe many thanks.

If it had not been for the Department for Education and Skills' Museums and Galleries Education Programme that provided the funding for the research post and the publication, this project would never have been realised. We are very grateful for their support.

The illustrations used are all copyright of Lambeth Archives with the following exceptions. Plate 1 is reproduced with permission of Lambeth Palace Library; Plate 2 is reproduced with permission of the President and Fellows of Magdalen College Oxford; Plates 4, 5, and 10 are reproduced with permission of the Corporation of London, London Metropolitan Archives; Plate 6 is reproduced with the permission of the British Library.

The single authorial voice is all too often a convenient fiction that conceals the work of many other individuals and this is certainly the case here. I must especially thank Howard Falksohn who had the initial idea for the research, the persistence to present it for funding and who went on to manage the project in its early stages. I need to thank Steve Martin and Elena Hahn who carried out the actual documentary research for 18 months, always with conviction and conscientiousness, and who have continued to promote the project ever since, and Steve Gray who has subsequently added to their work. Some previous researchers had already covered part of the ground before us and in particular I need to thank Sheila Gallagher and the East Surrey Family History Society for access to their Lambeth settlement examination indexes and John Brown of Local History Publications for the access he gave to his work on the Streatham parish records. Many other people have commented on or otherwise helped with the project as it progressed, and I would like to single out Julie Evans of the Casbah project, Sam Walker of Black Cultural Archives, Helen Wood of the Black and Asian Londoners project, Sean Creighton of BASA, Mike Philips of South Bank University and Hakim Adi of Middlesex University.

1   Parish Registers

The area now known as the London Borough of Lambeth was three distinct parishes in the eighteenth and nineteenth centuries, each with their own local administrations. The largest was the parish of St Mary Lambeth, immediately south of the City and Westminster, but separated from London proper by the river. In the late eighteenth century Lambeth's population started to increase dramatically as it gradually turned into a southern suburb of London. By contrast the two smaller parishes of Holy Trinity Clapham and St Leonard Streatham remained rural villages until late into the nineteenth century and were not so obviously part of London. Each of these three parishes has surviving registers of baptism, marriage and burial from the sixteenth century.

The detailed searches of the registers that we undertook revealed some interesting results both in terms of individual and demographic information about the black population of the three parishes and about the potential of parish registers as a general source. We recorded two different levels of finds. Definite finds, where the individual's race was clearly recorded as "black" "negro", "mulatto" etc., are transcribed chronologically by parish at the end of this chapter. Possible finds, where the register entry suggested that they might indicate a black or foreign person, have been included as Appendix One. Such "possibles" include unusual surnames, surnames that are frequently found as slave names, surnames that are possibly descriptive e.g. "Mr Blackmore", people described as "strangers" or references to a birth place in the Caribbean, Africa or elsewhere that do not specify the race of the person.

The search showed that baptism and, to a lesser extent, burial registers were good sources for recording the presence of black people. The Lambeth Clapham and Streatham baptism and burial registers contained a total of 80 identified black people for the period 1626 - 1812, together with a further 200 people identified as possible black people. The registers often gave additional information about individuals including age at baptism, the master's name where the person was a slave or a servant and occasionally the master's address. The parish priest was only required to list the names of the person being baptised and his or her parents and the date; any further information was his own choice. So it is interesting and helpful for our purposes that the descriptions of black people in these registers clearly benefited from their very visible ethnicity in a white society. This "otherness" was often recorded by the minister while the "otherness" of other newcomers to the parish - Huguenots, Irish or Germans for instance - was not remarked on.

While the evidence from the baptism and burial registers was good, the marriage registers, by contrast, gave us no information at all. A search of the St Mary Lambeth marriage register for the period 1669 - 1797 did not produce a single entry where the race or ethnicity of a person was identified, even though there were entries in the baptism register for the children of, presumably married, black parents. As a result we ceased searching in the marriage registers.

The baptism and burial registers became similarly "colour blind" after 1812 when an "Act for the better regulating and preserving Parish and other registers of baptism, marriage and burial in England" was passed. This imposed a standard printed register that all churches were obliged to use. The possibility for any descriptive extras on the part of the minister was now removed. Where previously he had written freehand in a volume and was able to add as much additional detail as he saw fit, now he was required to fill in the boxes on a pre-printed page. We continued to search the Lambeth baptism registers up until 1834 but the last definite find was in February 1812, just 5 months before the passing of the Act: the baptism of *Ann Elizabeth Marner, a negro woman about 30 years of age*. After 1812 Lambeth's black population cease to be recorded in any identifiable way in the registers. As a result we did not go on to search the nineteenth century registers of any of the new Lambeth parishes that were created in the 1820's; neither did we search any of the registers of non-conformist churches in Lambeth.

Our research identified other constraints on using parish registers. Baptism and to a lesser extent burial registers were clearly a useful source until 1812. But even before 1812 there was no actual requirement on the minister's part to record ethnic information. If it was only because black people were very visible in a white society that they were so described in the registers, then this perhaps helps explain why the burial registers did not record black people so frequently. Of the 80 confirmed register entries for black people in Lambeth, only thirteen were for burials. The black child or adult receiving baptism was physically there before the minister and was noted. Whereas the burial ceremony concealed the identity of the dead within a coffin and unless the person had been previously known to the minister his or her race seems to have often been ignored.

14

This doesn't provide an explanation for the complete absence of black marriages. Such events were highly visible affairs and even if they didn't make it into the registers, they were occasionally reported in the newspapers, presumably for their novelty value. An article in the Westminster paper *The St James' Evening Post* for 1726 described in detail the marriage of a "Guiney Black" and his wife. There were other factors that help explain this absence from the registers. Plantation slaves in the Caribbean were not allowed a Christian marriage and were accustomed to using informal or non-Christian ceremonies to confirm their partnerships. Black families were unusual in London in the eighteenth century. Some commentators have suggested that there were only two recorded married black couples in London in the eighteenth century - Ignatius Sancho and his wife and John and Mary Hylas.[4] Certainly the slave origins of London's black population meant that it was a predominantly male community. The evidence of the Lambeth registers seems to confirm this; 75% of the entries for men or boys. As a result black marriages would have been unusual and the normal partnership was a mixed one of a black man and a white woman. But such "miscegenation" was mostly viewed with distaste by eighteenth century English society (unlike plantation concubinage in the Caribbean where sexual relationships between white planter and black female slave were seen as an unexceptionable *droit de seigneur*). Such social disapproval may well have further discouraged couples from a formal marriage ceremony. There were also economic arguments; the marriage ceremony was not automatically used by poorer people and most poor blacks in London with their similarly disadvantaged white partners may simply have avoided the ceremony for that reason. [5]

This gender disproportion also helps explain why the London black population largely disappears from sight in the nineteenth century. The abolition in the nineteenth century of first the slave trade and then of slavery itself meant that the supply of new black people, previously brought over against their will as servant or slave by a white master, effectively ceased. If, as the parish registers suggest, it was only their blackness that was noteworthy, and if with a predominantly male black population most marriages were of necessity mixed-race unions, at what point did the subsequent generations - "mulatto", "quadroon" and "octoroon" - cease to be perceived as and recorded as

[4] *Letters of the Late Ignatius Sancho,* ed. Vincent Carretta, 1995 and
Black England, Gretchen Gerzina, 1995
[5] For instance the Hindoo beggar who testified to Henry Mayhew in the early 1860s, "I married that girl for some time. I have been married several times. I do not mean to say that I have ever been to church as rich folks do; but I have been married without that." *London Labour and London Poor* vol.IV, p.424

black? We see this happening in the Lambeth registers. *Mary Camell, a Black woman aged 23 years* was baptised in October 1793. Nine months later in July 1794 *Ann, daughter of William Marshall and Mary Camell* was also baptised.[6] Mary's baptism was probably the preliminary to if not marriage – it is not recorded in the Lambeth register - then at least an unofficial union with William Marshall who must have been white. For Ann - their mixed race offspring, baptised by the same minister who noted Mary's ethnicity nine months before - is not described as black.

There is a further question mark about the extent to which all black people in Lambeth would have had access to the baptism ceremony. Today baptism registers are the prosaic record of a standard rite of passage; in the eighteenth century they possessed considerably more significance for black slaves. The christianisation of slaves on British islands in the Caribbean had been fiercely resisted by white planters. The act of baptism implicitly recognised the existence of an individual before God. This religious identity was completely at odds with the slave laws operating in British plantations which defined slaves as chattels or property that had no legal existence as individuals. A key legal judgement in 1677 had stated that Negroes "being infidels there might be property in them". In the eighteenth century William Blackstone noted "the infamous and unchristian practice of withholding baptism from Negro servants, lest they should thereby gain there liberty".[7]

There was a considerable amount of uncertainty as to whether or not black slaves automatically acquired freedom when in England. This was tested through the eighteenth century in a series of contradictory and ambiguous court cases and was not fully resolved until the abolition of slavery in 1833. Many black slaves, like Olaudah Equiano, mistakenly believed that the rite of baptism was a way of obtaining liberty when in England, particularly when their masters had allowed the distinction between slavery and service to become blurred[8]. While many white masters were prepared to have individual black domestic servants or slaves baptised, it was a ceremony that they tended to retain control over. It was the reward for a favoured individual and would normally only take place with the masters permission and ministers would not

[6] St. Mary Lambeth baptism register; LMA/MRY1/P85/348

[7] *Commentaries on the Laws of England*, William Blackstone, 1765-1769

[8] For example Olaudah's confusion when his master sold him on to a new owner in 1762
"I told him my master could not sell me to him, nor to anyone else.......besides this I have been baptised; and by the laws of the land no man has the right to sell me. I added that I had heard a lawyer and others at different times tell my master so."
The Life of Olaudah Equiano pp. 58-9

normally baptise an adult black without first obtaining it. Far from being an automatic right, it was a ceremony that could be offered or withheld by the master and one that it might be dangerous or impossible for an escaped slave to obtain when in England.

All of these factors mean that the 80 confirmed results obtained from the registers have to be viewed as only a fraction of the real black population in Lambeth. Nevertheless, the results that we do have are substantial enough to draw some general conclusions about this community.

The earliest record of a black person in Lambeth is the baptism in 1626 of George Horsan, an Indian living at Lambeth Palace in the household of the Archbishop of Canterbury. The first black African is John the son of Abimelech Potter, "a blackamore" who was baptised in 1669. Most of the black people in the eighteenth century registers were slaves or domestic servants. It was common practice in the Caribbean to give slaves no surname and a number of the Lambeth baptisms perpetuate this practice. Many were being baptised later in life and were unsure of their exact age - suggesting a recent arrival and a prior, non-Christian life in Africa or the Caribbean. The absence of the names of parents for many of the children would also suggest that most had been orphaned by slavery or service. Some were described as the property of a master. The disproportionate number of black men was also a reminder of their recent slave origin, where male blacks were more attractive because stronger. Some of the names given at baptism were further reminders of slave status: William and Richard *Lambeth* baptised in 1774 and described as the servants of John Knott of Kennington Lane were an example of the common practice of naming slaves after a master or his place of residence. The burial of Obadiah January *, a poor black*, at Stockwell chapel in January 1784 suggests that he only acquired a surname as a casual afterthought when he died. By contrast, Robert *Freeman* baptised as an adult in 1749 was almost certainly a recently freed slave acquiring a heavily symbolic surname for the first time. Carlos, the black servant of Thomas Geils, baptised in 1781 received no surname and his slave or servant status was further reinforced by his position in the register at the end of a list of Geil's five children, all baptised on the same day (Pl.4).[9]

In addition to the official set of parish registers for St. Mary Lambeth an incomplete draft set of registers survives for some years. These were the rough register entries

---

[9] St. Mary Lambeth baptism register; LMA/MRY1/P85/343-348

made by the priest that were then used to write up the official record. Comparing the two registers is instructive as the draft entries sometimes contain additional information that has been edited out in the final version. The official baptism entry for George Blackmore on 30 Sept 1702 is recorded as: *George Blackmore a Negro about ye age of 12 years from St Martins in ye Fields* .The draft register gives a lot more: *George Blackmore a Negro about the age of 12 years belonging to Mr. Philips at the sign of the Castle near Beaufort Buildings in the parish of St Martins in the Fields* (Pl. 3).[10]

What can be unpicked from a very brief biographical note like this? It tells that Blackmore was the servant or slave of Mr Philips, the landlord of the Castle public house, Beaufort Buildings; significantly this was just off the Strand in Westminster and overlooked Lambeth across the river Thames. It doesn't explain why although living in a Westminster parish George was baptised in Lambeth, but it does serves as a nice paradigm for the suburban relationship between metropolitan Westminster and still largely rural Lambeth in the eighteenth century. In 1702 when twelve year old George Blackmore was sent to Lambeth parish church for his baptism he would have come by boat because there was no bridge. Links between the two parishes were by ferry; people from Westminster might come to visit the river-side pleasure gardens at Vauxhall, but there was little else in Lambeth to justify the boat trip. All this changed in 1751 with the construction of Westminster Bridge. This was the first new London river crossing for 600 years and was soon followed by Blackfriars Bridge in 1766. These new routes provided easy access to cheap land just across the river from crowded Westminster and prompted a development bonanza that saw Lambeth transform itself over the next 50 years from sleepy Surrey riverside village to brand new London suburb.

Westminster already possessed a significant black population. Slaves or freed black servants typically entered England for the first time through to London docks with their masters who would generally have their London residence in Westminster. Those blacks who were freed generally stayed in London where their colour and status were less of a hindrance to making a living and where there was already a proto-black community. At the end of the eighteenth century the black population of London was perceived as problematically large and estimated at anything between 3,000 and 20,000, the majority of whom lived in Westminster or around the docks in East London.

---

[10] St. Mary Lambeth draft baptism register, LAD/P9/2

The evidence in the Lambeth registers suggests that London's black population must have been one element of that suburban movement across the newly constructed bridges into Lambeth. There were eight confirmed references in the St Mary Lambeth baptism and burial registers to black people before 1752 when Westminster bridge opened. But in the sixty years from 1752 up until 1812, when the registers cease to note the ethnicity of people, there was a near five-fold increase with 38 such records of black people.

However, the limited extent of this suburban migration is shown by the results from the two other parishes that made up the present borough of Lambeth. Clapham and Streatham were further still from London and remained rural well into the nineteenth century. As a result while there is much evidence of London merchants whose wealth derived from sugar and slaves living in these parishes, there is far less evidence of a resident black population. There are just three references in the Streatham registers for the whole period, all of them to servants or slaves belonging to named masters. The figures for Clapham are skewed because of the presence of Zachary Macaulay's African Academy at the beginning of the nineteenth century. But if we exclude the baptisms and burials of blacks who came to Clapham to participate in that experiment then there are only five other earlier references to black people in that parish.

Macaulay's African Academy derived from his and Granville Sharpe's earlier and less successful experiment at resettling freed slaves in Sierra Leone in the 1780's. Macaulay returned to Clapham and in 1800 set up the Academy at his house on Clapham Common, with the support of the Church Missionary Society and the Clapham rector, John Venn. It's purpose was to educate and train free blacks from Sierra Leone as missionaries who would then return to their country. It was not an exclusively male enterprise; there were apparently four black girls also being educated, but as they were living at a house in the neighbouring parish of Battersea, they do not appear in the Clapham registers.[11]

The Holy Trinity registers record 18 baptisms and five burials for the years 1801 to 1805 and one earlier baptism in 1792 associated with the scheme. John Venn was a

---

[11] *John Venn and the Clapham Sect*, p.241

good friend of Macaulay and an enthusiastic supporter of the Academy experiment. [12] As a result his register entries are peculiarly detailed, giving age, status and often the precise part of Africa or the Caribbean that the students came from (Pl.5). Many came from different parts of Sierra Leone - the Bullom Shore, Rio Pongas in the Susoo country, Bananas and Logo in the Temne country are all specified. Others like John Thorp have their slave ancestry described, *a Maroon originally from the coast of Africa near the Gulf of Guinea – born in Jamaica.*

In contrast with the near anonymity of many of the Lambeth parish baptisms, where slaves and bonded servants were often acquiring a name and an independent existence for the first time, the students of the African Academy come well documented. Many were clearly from important families in Sierra Leone: the sons of chiefs, kings, traders and plantation owners. Perhaps this should not surprise us; the Church Missionary Society and Macaulay and Venn would have been keen to train up effective, powerful advocates to return to Sierra Leone; and what better than to use the sons of the existing ruling class?

One of these comes with a considerable historical baggage. Henry Granville Naimbana, described in the baptism register of 5 October 1792 as *an African from Sierra Leone* was in fact the son of Nembgana, often written Naimbana, who was regent of the Koya Kingdom from 1775 to 1793. He signed the treaty making way for the establishment of the British colony at Freetown and is now celebrated as one of the founding figures in Sierra Leone; his image appears on the 10 lei coin. He was a progressive ruler who was opposed to the slave trade and who had at least three of his sons educated abroad; two received a Christian education in France and England while a third received an Islamic education in North Africa.

Henry Granville Naimbana (actually John Frederick before he took a new baptised name in honour of his two patrons[13]) came to England from Sierra Leone in June 1791. His dress and his style of travel was in sharp contrast to that of most blacks who ended up in Lambeth in the eighteenth century. *The Prince was decorated in an old*

---

[12] The baptisms on May 12 1805 were attended by William Wilberforce, Zachariah Macaualy, Henry Thornton and others; John Venn preached the sermon. *John Venn and the Clapham Sect*, p.242

[13] Granville Sharp was an important abolitionist of the late eighteenth century who did much to test the legality of slavery in Britain through the courts. With Zachary Macaulay he founded the Sierra Leone Company in 1792. He lived briefly on Clapham Common.

blue cloak, bound with broad gold lace: which with a black velvet coat, pair of white satin breeches, a couple of shirts and two or three pairs of trowsers form a compleat inventory of his stock of cloaths when he left Africa. Granville Sharp and Henry Thornton were his patrons in England, oversaw his education, got him baptised at Clapham and commissioned an oil portrait of the Prince that was sent to his father. He was also the subject of an improving tract, *The Black Prince* which described his time in England (Pl. 6). But in February 1793 King Naimbana died in Sierra Leone and his son returned home. Contracting a fever on the ship, he wrote his will and died just as the boat reached Sierra Leone.[14]

There was a curious sequel to this royal African link with Clapham; the last identified black baptisms in the parish are those of John and William Comassee in 1836, guests of William Dunbar and both described as Kings of Ashantee in present-day Ghana[15].

The Academy was generally reckoned as an honourable failure; the Clapham registers record not just the influx of newly baptised young black boys and men from Africa and Jamaica, but also the high mortality rate that was one of the main reason for the project's failure. Only six survived the climate and diseases of England to return to Sierra Leone. Two of the deaths during the 1802 measles epidemic that affected the Academy provide an interesting footnote to black migration in the late eighteenth century. William Small and George Kizell are both described in the burial register as of the African Academy and born in Nova Scotia in Canada. There was indeed a significant black settlement in Nova Scotia; many of the servants and freed slaves of the white settlers who remained loyal to England during the American War of Independence fled to Canada after 1784. At least two of their offspring appear to have died of measles and been buried in a South London churchyard as a result of Zachary Macaulay's good-intentioned experiment.

There is an important difference between the baptismal records of the Clapham African Academy students and those for other the black people in Lambeth. John Venn's register for the period 1802 -1805 provides a detailed and, ultimately, self

---

Henry Thornton was MP for Southwark . He shared a house on Clapham Common with William Wiberforce and it was there that most of the meetings of the Clapam Sect took place.
[14] *Prince Niambana In England* , Sierra Leone Studies, No. 8, 1957
The Black Prince, a True Story being an Account of the Life and Death of Naimabanna, an African King's son who arrived in England in the Year 1791 and set sail on his return in June 1793,
[15] Holy Trinity Clapham baptism register, LMA/P95/TRI1/091-092

serving record of the philanthropic actions of his friends in the Clapham Sect. That is why we have been left with so much extraordinary detail about the pedigrees of these future black missionaries. The other Lambeth registers are much less self-conscious in the way they record the young black slaves and bonded servants brought to church by their owners for baptism. Yet for all their brevity and in spite of their failure to systematically record all the black people who may have been here, they provide us with an invaluable starting point for assessing Lambeth's earliest black community.

St Mary Lambeth Registers for Baptism & Burial

George Horsan an Indian dwelling wth ye Lo: Arch Bp of Cant his Grace being presented at the ffour by Dcor Harns & Dcor Jefreys Chaplaines in House & after the Indian had made his confession of ffaith & Craving to be Baptised,was by Dcor ffeatly then Rector named Georg.	31 Dec1626	MRY1/P85/341
John the sonne of Abimelech Potter a blackamore	4 Apr 1669	MRY1/P85/341
St Mary's Lambeth baptism: Thomas Springs a blackamore supposed to bee about Eight Yeares of age	29 Mar 1674	MRY1/P85/343
St Mary's Lambeth baptism: George Blackmore a Negro about ye age of 12 years from St Martins in ye Fields [16]	30 Sep 1702	MRY1/P85/343
St Mary's Lambeth burials: a Blackmoore	13 Oct 1719	MRY1/P85/344
St Mary's Lambeth burials: Samuel, son of Samuel a Blackmore	5 Mar 1722	MRY1/P85/344
St Mary's Lambeth baptism: Richard Morris, a Black about 20 years of age	25 Oct 1729	MRY/P85/344
St Mary's Lambeth baptism: Robert Freeman, an adult Black born 16th March 1712	12 Apr 1749	MRY1/P85/345
Samuel Sampson, a Black 23 years old when baptised	15 Jul 1752	MRY/1/P85/345
St Mary's Lambeth burials: Joanna Maria, a negro	22 Aug 1766	MRY1/P85/346
St Mary's Lambeth baptism: William Whalley, a negro supposed to be 17 yrs	17 Nov 1767	MRY1/P85/346
St Mary's Lambeth baptism: Durham Butler, a Black said to be 20 years old	25 June 1768	MRY1/P85/346
St Mary's Lambeth baptism: Chas Hunt a Negro (abt. 8 Years old) sert. to Mr. Wood	22March17	MRY1/85/346
John Essex a Negro aged 19 years	28 May 1773	MRY1/85/346
Wm. Lambeth (aged 15 yrs) Negro Servants to Jno Knott Esqr. [17]	4 Sept 1774	MRY1/85/346
Richd. Lambeth (aged 15 yrs) Negro Servants to Jno Knott Esqr. [18]	4 Sept 1774	MRY1/85/346

[16] The draft baptism register gives a much fuller description, "George Blackmore a Negro about the age of 12 years belonging to Mr. Philips at the sign of the Castle near Beaufort Buildings in the parish of St Martins in the Fields"   LAD/P9/2

[17] The draft baptism register gives a fuller description, "Wm. Lambeth. A Black Boy aged 15 years. Servant to John Knott Esqr. In Kennington Lane"   LAD/P9/4A

St Mary's Lambeth baptism: George Wilkinson, a black aged 26 years	17 May 1777	MRY1/P8 5/347
St Mary's Lambeth baptism: Henry Martin, a black aged 26 years	28 Nov 1777	MRY1/P8 5/347
St Mary's Lambeth baptism: James Francis, a black aged 15 years	11 Nov 1778	MRY1/P8 5/347
St Mary's Lambeth baptism: Thomas Magams, a black aged 18 years	7 Jan 1781	MRY1/P8 5/347
St Mary's Lambeth baptism: Carlos a black servant to Thomas Geils aged 18 years[19]	8 Sep 1781	MRY1/P8 5/347
St Mary's Lambeth baptism: Edward Furguson, a black aged 22 years	1 Jan 1782	MRY1/P8 5/347
St Mary's Lambeth baptism: Clara Garrick, a black woman aged 29 years	22 Oct 1783	MRY1/P8 5/347
Stockwell Chapel burial: Obadiah January, a black, poor	13 Jan 1784	MRY1/P8 5/347
St Mary's Lambeth baptism: Frederick Peter Ginlick, a black aged 18 years	14 Nov 1784	MRY1/P8 5/347
St Mary's Lambeth baptism: Frances Cuneffe (sp ?), a black aged 17	7 Oct 1785	MRY1/P8 5/347
St Mary's Lambeth baptism: Samuel Allen a black aged 19 years	5 Sep 1786	MRY1/P8 5/347
St Mary's Lambeth burials: Matilda, a Black woman – High St.	30 Dec 1789	MRY1/P8 5/348
St Mary's Lambeth baptism: James Foster, a Black aged 25 years	9 May 1790	MRY1/P8 5/348
St Mary's Lambeth baptism: William Hope a Black aged 19 years	28 Jul 1793	MRY1/P8 5/348
St Mary's Lambeth baptism: Mary Camell a Black woman aged 23 years	30 Oct 1793	MRY1/P8 5/348
St Mary's Lambeth baptism: Ann –daughter of William Marshall and Mary Camell[20]	11 Jul 1794	MRY1/P8 5/348
St Mary's Lambeth baptism: Ann Alfred a negro woman aged 30 years	10 Aug 1794	MRY1/P8 5/348

[18] The draft baptism register gives a much fuller description, "Richard Lambeth. A Black Boy aged 15 years. Servant to John Knott Esqr. In Kennington Lane"   LAD/P9/4A

[19] The baptism of Carlos took place on the same day as the that of the four sons and one daughter of Thomas and Mary Geils, aged 7, 6, 4, 3 and 1. They appear in the register in order of age followed by Carlos.

[20] Although Ann is not described as black she is clearly the daughter of Mary Camell who was baptised in October 1793

St Mary's Lambeth baptism: Philip Devergne son of Philip Devergne and a West India woman (name unknown) born 15 Jul 1791	18 Jul 1798	MRY1/P8 5/349
St Mary's Lambeth baptism: Thomas Smith, a black boy about 15 years	10 Oct 1798	MRY1/P8 5/349
St Mary's Lambeth baptism: George Phippin, a black aged 19 years	19 Feb 1800	MRY1/P8 5/349
St Mary's Lambeth baptism: Caesar Smart, a black born in Bombay, East Indies (1789)	26 Dec 1800	MRY1/P8 5/349
St Mary's Lambeth baptism: Richard Carrie (sp!!), a black aged 20 years	7 May 1801	MRY1/P8 5/349
St Mary's Lambeth baptism: Louisa Phillips, a black born in Africa aged 20 years	2 Sep 1803	MRY1/P8 5/349
Stockwell Chapel baptism: Cunicibuch of William and Lais Piper born 1803	10 Jun 1804	MRY1/P8 5/349
St Mary's Lambeth baptism: William Thomas, a black man aged 24 years	6 Aug 1806	MRY1/P8 5/349
St Mary's Lambeth baptism: William Clarke, a black man about 21 years of age	24 Oct 1806	MRY1/P8 5/349
St Mary's Lambeth baptism: James Knight about 12 years of age a negro	19 Oct 1808	MRY1/P8 5/349
St Mary's Lambeth baptism: Mary Ann Russell, a black woman, aged 21 years	3 Oct 1810	MRY/P85/ 349
St Mary's Lambeth baptism: Ann Elizabeth Marner, a negro woman about 30 years of age	9 Feb 1812	MRY/P85/ 349
St Mary's Lambeth baptism: Xavier son of/ Jose & Marie/ - - / Brookstreet/ the people called " the Indian Chaps" natural of Brazil	28 May 1822	MRY1/P8 5/353

St Leonard Streatham & Holy Trinity Clapham Registers for Baptism and Burial

St Leonards Streatham burials Pick, a negro man at Mr Chaplins	1695		P95/LEN
St. Leonard's Streatham baptism Joseph Steel }two adult Negroes	6 1717	Jun	P95/LEN/ 062
St. Leonard's Streatham baptism William Steel } two adult Negroes	6 1717	Jun	P95/LEN/ 062
Holy Trinity Clapham baptism: No 27 John, a Black Boy belonging to Mrs. Martin	29 1733	Sept	P95/ TR11/090
Holy Trinity Clapham baptism: No 17 Christopher Sheppard - a Black Adult	8 1761	Mar	P95/ TR11/090
Holy Trinity Clapham baptism: No17 Robert Jackson, an adult Black 25	25 1776	Aug	P95/ TRI1/091/ 001
Holy Trinity Clapham baptism: No 68 Henry Granville Naimbana, an African from Sierra Leone[21]	5 1792	Oct	P95/ TRI1/091/ 001
Holy Trinity, Clapham baptism: No.31 Elizabeth Gaudie, wife of James Guadie, late Blackmore spinster	19 1795	Apr	P95/ TRI1/091/ 001
Holy Trinity, Clapham burial: John Cranbrook – married man – a mulatto greengrocer aged 46 years	13 1797	Jul	P95/ TRI1/091/ 001
Holy Trinity, Clapham baptism No.94: Issac Watt aged about 15 yrs, the son of an African heathen. Parents living in the kingdom of Foy (sp?) in Africa. Educated at the African Academy in this parish.	19 1801	Oct	P95/ TRI1/091/ 001
Holy Trinity Clapham burial No.50: William Small – aged 17 yrs of the African School. Born in Nova Scotia – measles[22]	1 1802	Jun	P95/ TRI1/091/ 001

---

[21] This is a son of King Naimbana of Sierra Leone. The name Henry Granville is in honour of his two Clapham patrons, Granville Sharpe and Henry Thornton.

[22] Although Nova Scotia is in Canada there was a large black settlement there after 1783 comprising refugees from the American war of Independence and from the failed Sierra Leone resettlement

Holy Trinity, Clapham burial No.57: George Kizell (of the African School) son of John Kizell, aged 12 yrs , born in Nova Scotia – measles	22 Jun 1802	P95/ TRI1/091/ 001
Holy Trinity Clapham David Fantimance – an African from Sierra Leone, educating at the African Academy in this parish. Aged about 13 yrs.	15 Jul 1802	Hol Trin Clapham Burial:72
Holy Trinity, Clapham, baptism No.82 William Bannah aged 15 yrs – son of Naimbannah the deputy of Turama (sp?) King of the Temne country	31 Jul 1802	P95/ TRI1/091/ 001
Holy Trinity, Clapham baptism No.83: Joseph William (Ka Fodee) – aged 15 yrs from Wangapong, a town in the Susoo country – son of Ka Fode, a chief in the Rokelle	31 Jul 1802	P95/ TRI1/091/ 001
Holy Trinity, Clapham baptism No.84: Peter Smith (Pa Dick) – aged 15 from the Bullom Shore, son of Pa Dick and nephew to Pa Jack who visited England in 1791	31 Jul 1802	P95/ TRI1/091/ 001
Holy Trinity, Clapham baptism No.85 William Tamba aged 12, Son of Pa Tamba a trader from the Bullam Shore	31 July 1802	P95/ TRI1/091/ 001
Holy Trinity, Clapham baptism No.86: James Fantimance (Foree Carree) – aged 10, son of Foree Carree, trader from the Bullom Shore, now resident at Makandee in the Susoo country	31 Jul 1802	P95/ TRI1/091/ 001
Holy Trinity, Clapham baptism No.130: John Macauley – son of Pa Jack an African chief of the Bullom Shore near Sierra Leone	21 Dec 1802	P95/ TRI1/091/ 001
Holy Trinity, Clapham burial No.2: Thomas Carr – an African youth from the Bullom Shore, aged about 16 yrs	8 Jan 1803	P95/ TRI1/091/ 001
Holy Trinity Clapham baptism No.58: William Fantimance – son of a chief of the Rio Pongas in the Susoo country	10 Mar 1805	P95/TRI 1/092
Holy Trinity Clapham baptism No.59: Lory Goloram – Son of Duke Goloram in the Rio Pongas in the Susoo country	3 May 1805	P95/TRI 1/092
Holy Trinity Clapham baptism No.66: Stephen George Calker – Son of Stephen Calker, proprietor of the plantations and other islands near Sierra Leone 16 or 17	12 May 1805	P95/TRI 1/092
Holy Trinity Clapham baptism No.67: John Calker – son of Stephen Calker. 10 or 12	12 May 1805	P95/TRI 1/092

Holy Trinity, Clapham baptism No.68: Yarrah – son of Naminamodoo a chief of the port Logo (sp?) in the Temne country. 17 yrs	12 1805	May	P95/TRI 1/092
Holy Trinity, Clapham baptism No.69: Samuel Peter – son of Tomro (sp?) a near relation of Pa Jack (now King George Bann) of Yongroo (sp?) on the Bullom Shore – about 14 yrs old	12 1805	May	P95/TRI 1/092
Holy Trinity, Clapham baptism No.70: Caesar Russell – son of Boora on the Bullom Shore	12 1805	May	P95/TRI 1/092
Holy Trinity, Clapham baptism No.71: John Thorp – son of John Thorp a Maroon originally from the coast of Africa near the Gulf of Guinea – born in Jamaica – about 15 yrs	12 1805	May	P95/TRI 1/092
Holy Trinity, Clapham, baptism No.72: Thomas Smith – son of Andrew Smith, a Maroon originating from the same part of Africa – born in Jamaica – about 17 yrs	12 1805	May	P95/TRI 1/092
Holy Trinity, Clapham baptism No.73: James – son of Bubucorree near the Rio Pongas in the Susoo country	12 1805	May	P95/TRI 1/092
Holy Trinity, Clapham baptism No.96: Bolsey (sp?) Fowles – An African aged 20 yrs from Bananas near Sierra Leone	13 1805	Jul	P95/TRI 1/092
Holy Trinity, Clapham burial No.57: Bolsey (sp?) Fowles – an African from Bananas near Sierra Leone	18 1805	Jul	P95/TRI 1/120
Holy Trinity, Clapham burial No.2: Catherine (?) Willow – a spinster , Black servant to Col. Lys (?) 20 yrs old	9 1813	Jan	P95/TRI 1/120
Holy Trinity, Clapham baptism No 1 John Tootoo Quamina Comassee, King of Ashantee, William Dunbar Rt.	28 1836	Oct	P95/TRI1/ 095/001
Holy Trinity, Clapham baptism William Accootoo Comassee, King of Ashantee, Wm. Dunbar Rt	28 1836	Oct	P95/TRI1/ 095/001

2   Poor Law Records

From what was already known about London's larger black community it seemed probable that many black people in Lambeth would also be poor or in need. To be in employment and earning a wage was seen as a certificate of free status and entitlement. The traditional route to employment and to a trade was through the system of apprenticeship. Yet black people were specifically excluded from this avenue. In 1736 for instance the City of London had barred blacks from serving apprenticeships to any of the city trades.[23] Domestic service was the only work that black people were sought out for. Many black Londoners trying to operate outside that tightly defined arena of legitimate employment were inevitably pushed into other activities: as beggars, street musicians, petty thieves and prostitutes. They must also have needed regular access to charity and relief.

In one sense their experiences cannot have been dissimilar to those of the existing white urban underclass, but with the added dimensions of race and, for first generation blacks, the problem of their lack of legal "settlement". The assistance available to the poor of the eighteenth century was provided either by the local parish or by public charities. Parish charities defined eligibility by whether or not a claimant lived in the parish and had a "settlement". The main type of parish charity was the statutory poor law relief that a parish had to make to poor people living there. But there were also various parochial charities set up by individual bequests that established their own rules about eligibility. Most of these parochial charities specifically excluded people who had already applied to the parish for poor relief. Public charities were often set up to address a specific need - orphans, blind people, prostitutes - and raised their own funds and wrote their own rules. Many London public charities were based in Lambeth at this time.

The poor laws derived from sixteenth century legislation that made the care of poor people the responsibility of their local parish, and gave each parish powers to collect a rate to fund this. The system was administered by the church wardens whose accounts typically itemised every payment made against the rates. Prior to 1834 these record the payments of "out-relief" made to paupers in the parish. Out- or "out-door" relief payments were small sums of money paid weekly to individuals to buy food and clothing; the other available option was "indoor relief" where a pauper was sent to the parish's work house. It was these church wardens' accounts that was the first series of poor law records that we searched. However there were at least two factors that reduced their potential value as a source.

First, it would be extremely unlikely for slaves to be identified in the church wardens' accounts. Prior to the 1833 abolition of slavery they would still have been legally the property of their master and owner; and he rather than the parish would have been responsible for their upkeep. The second problem was that while it was possible that freed or runaway slaves or former servants might have been able to apply for out-relief, they would be likely to have fallen foul of the laws of settlement that governed poor law payments. These determined that a parish was only responsible for those paupers who had a legal right of settlement. Settlement was obtained by being born, owning or renting property, serving an apprenticeship or working as a servant in a parish. The settlement laws were specifically designed to exclude beggars or itinerants from elsewhere. Therefore it was likely that many blacks, in spite of their poverty, would have been so excluded because their transient status denied them such a settlement

The problem for black people lacking a settlement is supported by the evidence of *Vagabondia* , a published account of famous London beggars that appeared in 1817, which included descriptions of two black beggars: Joseph Johnson who had been a sailor and Charles McGee, a freed slave from Jamaica. Significantly they were both described as "having no claim to relief in any parish".[24] In other words they had been forced into begging because the settlement laws meant that they were the responsibility of no parish and could obtain no poor relief. By the mid-nineteenth century the negro and Hindu beggars had become a regular component of London street life, the subject of both casual journalism and more serious enquiry. Negro beggars were seen as particularly sympathetic objects of charity because of the popular support for the anti-slavery campaigns; so much so, as Henry Mayhew noted *That many white beggars, fortunate enough to possess a flattish or turned-up nose,*

---

[23] Court of Common Council records
[24] John Thomas Smith, *Vagabondia. Or Anecdotes of mendicant Wanderers through the Streets of London*, 1817

dyed themselves black and "stood pad" as real Africans. The imposture, however, was soon detected and punished. [25]

What was found in the Lambeth church wardens' accounts seemed to confirm the difficulties that black people must have experienced with poor relief. Apart from one remarkable exception, the accounts for the 120 year period from 1716 to 1834 contained no evidence of payments to black people. This was in spite of the evidence in the parish registers that showed at least forty black people being baptised or buried for the same period. The one exception was a period from 1719 to 1726 when four different black people living in Lambeth were simultaneously on poor relief (pl. 9). These were John Duke (a servant to a Mr Fox), Henry Mundox (another servant), "the black woman at Brixton Causeway" and an anonymous orphan known as "the Barbary child". The detail in the individual accounts allows us to reconstruct the bare elements of their lives in Lambeth. In October 1722 both Duke and Mundox fell ill, apparently with smallpox, and were admitted to hospital; Mundox recovered but Duke died and was laid out and buried in May 1723[26]. Meanwhile "the black woman at Brixton Causeway" had a bastard child in November 1722 and this has to be nursed up until February 1723. While this is going on there are also regular payments to "the Barbary child", presumably a sick pauper orphan, who receives intermittent payments of 6d per week between 1719 - 1726.

Four black paupers in a parish is hardly a statistical sample; but the fact that they were all simultaneously claiming relief is intriguing. Even this small sample seems to confirm the evidence of the parish registers where only a quarter of the entries described as black were for women and is another reminder of the recent slave origins of the black population. What is interesting about the church wardens' description of the one woman - "the black woman at Brixton Causeway" - is the way it suggests she could almost have been the only black woman in Lambeth at the time and so unusual a presence that she didn't even need to have a name; her colour and her location alone were enough to define her. Brixton Causeway was the present Brixton Road; in the early eighteenth century it was an open coach road running through fields from Kennington to Brixton Hill; a fairly desolate spot with almost no houses and only the occasional coaching inn. Quite how the woman lived, where she went after her bastard

[25] Charles Dickens, *Household Words* 22 May 1852; Henry Mayhew *London Labour and the London Poor* vol.IV, pp.423-6

[26] John Duke's burial is not recorded in the Lambeth burial register; it is likely that the hospital he went to was St. Thomas's, then in the parish of Southwark.

child was nursed or whether she stayed living by the side of the coach road, we do not know. But she was clearly briefly remarkable and is curiously suggestive of another solitary black woman living on the edge of London at the same time whose unusual presence ended up in her being enshrined as a local place name. "Black Mary's Hole" was a lonely spot on the road from London to Hampstead near Cold Bath Fields and was so named after *a Blackamoor woman called Mary, who about thirty years ago lived by the side of the road near the stile in a small circular hut built with stones.*[27]

Yet this one-off sequence of accounts recording payments to four poor blacks is problematic. If there were that many black paupers in Lambeth in the 1720s, then why is the increase in the black population - shown in the Lambeth baptism registers for the second half of the eighteenth century and generally noted throughout London - not reflected in the later church wardens' accounts? The incidence of runaway slaves and poor blacks in London increased throughout the century. Indeed by 1786 the Committee for the Relief of Black Poor - initially a private charity but subsequently taken over by central government - was set up specifically to deal with the problem in London with food distribution centres in Westminster and East London.

There are a couple of possible explanations, both of which highlight the unreliability of these records as a useful measure of the size of the black community. One plausible explanation is that an individual church warden, during his period of office in the 1720's, was struck by the fact that there were black people in the parish and chose to record them as such. We can assume that successor church wardens saw similar if not increasing numbers of black people but for some reason chose not to distinguish them from any other paupers receiving out-relief. In other words, apart from one brief interlude, the poor law records are "colour blind". Another possible explanation follows on from this; if the black population in Lambeth did increase during the century then its perceived status might change from one of being a novelty worthy of particular note in the records to that of a significant and worrying drain on the poor relief resources of the parish. It would also be one that the parish authorities could exclude by rigorously enforcing the settlement laws. There is certainly anecdotal evidence from elsewhere in London of church wardens moving on itinerant blacks or having them imprisoned rather than incur expenditure on them [28]. The post-1785 influx of newly freed blacks from America (accompanying their white former masters who had fought on the losing

---

[27] Elizabeth Helm, *London and its Environs Described*, 1761 (cited in Gerzina, *Black England* p.28)
[28] See Gerzina, *Black England* p.128.

side in the American War of Independence) saw many London parishes making rigorous use of vagrancy laws 1786-7 to arrest or move on poor blacks.

Whatever the explanation it is clear that there were briefly a number of black people receiving poor relief in Lambeth in the early eighteenth century and it is likely that there were yet more pauper blacks in later years that, for whatever reason, the records conceal. This suspicion is further confirmed by the almost completely negative evidence of the Lambeth parish settlement examinations. These examinations, carried out before a magistrate, record the biographical details of claimants for poor relief in order to establish whether or not they had a legal settlement and entitlement to poor relief. The surviving Lambeth sequence runs from 1780 - 1858 and contains over 19,000 individual examinations.[29] There are two separate sequences, one for the ordinary parish applicants and another for the applicants to the Lying-in Hospital at Lambeth which was an early hospital providing maternity help for expectant mothers from across London.[30] Within these 19,000 records over an 80 year period there are just two that refer to black people, both for women about to give birth at the Lying-in hospital. These scanty finds provide two brief accounts that were undoubtedly typical of black women's experiences in London.

Sarah Poleson was examined in September 1790; she was the daughter of a black slave in Jamaica and was still the property of her owner, John Gray who had brought her to England some years before to work as his servant in Tottenham. She had become pregnant and her master had moved her into lodgings in Lambeth so that she was eligible for the lying in hospital where she had given birth to an illegitimate child. Reading between the lines Sarah was probably a bonded servant rather than a slave; Gray's actions were relatively benign; he provided her with a letter of admission to the hospital and moved her to Lambeth so that she was close to the hospital. Perhaps he was the father of the child or Sarah was his illegitimate daughter? Neither possibility would have been unusual. For the magistrate hearing the examination, Sarah was not

---

[29] In fact it continues beyond that date. 1858 is the point to which the East Surrey Family History Society have got with their transcription and indexing of these records.

[30] The Westminster New Lying-in Hospital, subsequently the General Lying-in Hospital opened in Westminster Bridge Road, Lambeth in 1767. It was a charitable institution providing for "the relief of those child-bearing women who are the wives of poor industrious tradesmen or distressed housekeepers"; it was available to all London parishes. Because of this the Lambeth authorities were immediately concerned at the influx of impoverished mothers and illegitimate children who could become a charge to the parish. From 1773 an act required all mothers to be married or, if they were not, to notify the parish so that their circumstances and settlement could be examined.

a problem, her position as Gray's servant and residence elsewhere mean that if anything went wrong and the baby was abandoned it would have become the responsibility of Tottenham parish (Pl. 10).

By contrast Harriet Lane's experience at the same lying in hospital in March 1822 was considerably more brusque. She too was seeking admission to give birth, but unlike Sarah she was married and lived in Southwark. She had been born in Barbados, was probably a freed slave, but "has never gained a settlement in this country". The information about Harriet was cut short and the examination not proceeded with because the magistrate concluded that Harriet's evidence should be "not taken in consequence of H. Lane being a black woman and not knowing the nature of an oath". This is all the more puzzling given Harriet's apparent settled and married status; presumably unlike Sarah she lacked an influential patron or master to write a letter of admission on her behalf.

The magistrate's refusal to proceed with this examination might initially look like some sort of casual racism. In fact it is a rather more complex reminder of the uncertain legal status of slaves in England and the unresolved issue as to whether the slave laws created specifically for Caribbean and American colonies should also apply at home. Black slaves had no existence before the law in the West Indies. They could not plead a civil case and if they were the victims of criminal acts by white masters or overseers they could get no redress at law. Their "chattel" status enabled slaves to be purchased as goods and bequeathed in wills as property from one person to another. The magistrate here appears to have been making that assumption: Harriet Lane could only be a slave and, having no status as an individual at law, was not therefore capable of swearing an oath. We can assume that as a result Harriet was also denied access to the hospital to give birth.

One of the effects of Lambeth's transformation into southern suburb of London was that it could provide cheap locations for many London charities while keeping the inmates at arms-length from the respectable citizens of Westminster and the City. In addition to the Lying-in hospital many other London public charities chose Lambeth for their operations. The Female Orphan Asylum, the Magdalen Hospital for Penitent Prostitutes and the Bedlam Asylum all set up in or relocated to Lambeth and Blackfriars in the late eighteenth and early nineteenth centuries. The Lying-in hospital did not officially exclude black people, although the negative evidence of our research suggests that it was probably quite difficult for black women to get access. However, many of these other institutions, drawing up rules and regulations in the late eighteenth century within the context of a visibly growing black population in London and in Lambeth, quite specifically excluded black people because of their race.[31]

Apart from the poor law and the relief offered by public charities there were also many small parochial charities that would provide small gifts of money, food, coal and occasional gifts of warm clothing to the needy. There were over forty such charities in Lambeth parish alone, set up as individual bequests and administered by the church wardens. However these too can be disregarded as a source of information on the black presence as their strict rules on entitlement operated in a similar way to the laws of settlement in excluding all but local inhabitants of the parish. Most of these charities distinguished between the "deserving poor" who were eligible and the "abject poor" which included anyone who had already applied to the parish for poor relief – who were excluded. Because they were the gifts of local worthies they also tended to be further restricted by the prejudices and assumptions of the donors. Like the Turbeville charity that provided apprenticeships annually for the sons of poor Lambeth parishioners but excluded Roman Catholics, chimney sweeps and water men.

On the evidence here it is clear that poor law and charity records are not reliable indicators of a black presence. The occasional insights that they offer are interesting and, in the case of the settlement examinations, give some unusual biographical detail. Other sources show that there were a large number of black people in Lambeth who may have attempted to obtain poor relief. But it is also clear that the constraints of the settlement laws, uncertain perceptions of black people's legal status, the "colour-blindness" of much of the record keeping and the specific exclusions engineered by many charities all meant that this presence remained almost completely concealed. John Duke, Henry Mundox, the black woman of Brixton Causeway and Sarah Poleson are but occasional sightings of what must have been a much larger black underclass then living in Lambeth. In Harriet Lane's aborted settlement examination we catch a telling glimpse of the authorities in the actual act of exclusion of a black person; an experience that was undoubtedly all too common and yet rarely recorded.

---

[31] The Female Orphan Asylum in Westminster Bridge Road, set up "to preserve friendless and deserted girls from those dangers and misfortunes to which their distressed situation exposes them" admitted girls between the ages of 9 to12 years old and bound them apprentice at age 15 for seven years "as domestic servants in reputable families" Its rules specifically stated " no negro or mulatto girl to be admitted". Ducarel, *History and Antiquities of the Parish of Lambeth*, p. 104.

Lambeth church wardens' accounts 1719 - 1726

	LAD P1/2
Paid Barbary Child -/-/6	21 Feb 1719
Paid Barbary Child being sick 1 *s*.	14 Nov 1719
Paid Barbary child 6 *d*.	21 Feb 1720
Paid Barbary child 6 *d*.	5 Mar 1720
Paid Barbary child 6 *d*.	29 Mar 1720
Paid Barbary child 6 *d*.	31 Mar 1720
Paid Barbary child 6 *d*.	7 Apr 1720
Paid Barbary child 6 *d*.	11 Apr 1720
Paid Duke Mr Fox's Black being sick 1*s*.	11 Oct 1722
Paid the Black woman at Brixton Causeway 1*s*.	3 Nov 1722
Paid John Duke being sick 1*s*.	11 Nov 1722
Paid getting John Duke & Henry Mundox 2 Blacks into Hospitall 10*s*.	18 Oct 1722
Paid for a shirt & 2 weeks lodging for John Duke 3*s*. 6*d*.	18 Oct 1722
Paid for John Duke being sick	13 Dec 1722
Paid for Henry Mondux's [sic?] washing in the Hospital	13 Dec 1722
Paid nursing the Black woman's Bastard child 4*s*.	15 Dec 1722
Paid nursing the Black woman's child 3*s*.	22 Dec 1722
Paid for a shirt for Henry Mondux in the Hosptl. 2*s*.6 *d*.	27 Dec 1722
Paid the Black woman's child 2*s*.	29 Dec 1722
Paid nursing the Black woman's child 2*s*.	7 Jan 1723
Paid nursing the Black woman's child 2*s*.	12 Jan 1723
Paid nursing the Black woman's child as before 2*s*.	19 Jan 1723
Paid nursing the Black woman's child 2*s*.	2 Feb 1723
Paid nursing the Black woman's child 2 weeks 4*s*.	16 Feb 1723
Paid for her [Mary Amey see prev. entry] washing and Henry Mundox 5 weeks in Ditto [hospital] 2*s*. 6 *d*.	16 Feb 1723
Paid Henry Mundox Discharged from Hospl.1*s*.	21 Mar 1723
Paid for Henry Mundox washing 5 weeks 1*s*. 3*d*.	23 Mar 1723
Paid John Duke the Black being very bad	5 May 1723

2*s*.

Paid John Duke ye Black as before 2*s*.6*d*.	11 May 1723
Paid laying out John Duke 2*s*.	16 May 1723
Paid for nursing and lodging John Duke 2*s*.	16 May 1723
Paid the bearers fetching him [John Duke] 2*s*.	18 May 1723
Rec. of the Black woman in part of what I paid for nursing her bastard child 11*s*.[32]	18 Feb 1723
Paid Mr Jones what he laid out for Black Duke and a travelling woman and 3 children with smallpox 6*s*.	17 Jul 1723
Paid Barbary child being sick 6*d*.	23 Mar 1724
Paid Barbary child being sick 6*d*.	25 Mar 1724
By cash for ye Barbary child sick and poor 1*s*. 6*d*.	30 Mar 1724
Paid Barb. child sick 1*s*.	14 Apr 1724
Paid Bab. child sick 1*s*.	19 Apr 1724
Paid Bab. child sick 1*s*.	26 Apr 1724
Paid Bab. child sick 1*s*.	1 May 1724
Paid Bab. child sick 1*s*.	17 May 1724
Paid Bab. child sick 6 *d*.	12 Jun 1724
Paid Bab. child sick 6 *d*.	23 Jul 1724
Paid Bab. child sick 1 *s*.	30 Jul 1724
Paid Bab. child sick 1 s. 6 *d*.	2 Oct 1724
Paid Bab. child poor 1 *s*.	6 Oct 1724
Paid Bab. child Poor 6 *d*.	1 Mar 1726
Paid Bab. child sick 1 *s*.	25 May 1726

---

[32] title of document: Jonathan Chillwell Dto to Cash p. 131 v

Lambeth Settlement Examinations, 1790 - 1822

Sarah Poleson, a single woman, "that she was born of a Negro woman, the property of John Gray in the island of Jamaica, that he the said John Gray brought her, this examinant, as his servant from Jamaica to the kingdom of Great Britain and she continued in his service for several years together in Great Britain, the last year or thereabouts of which service she lived with him in the parish of Tottenham in the county of Middlesex, that then she proving with child her said master took her to a lodging in the said parish of St Mary Lambeth for two months before her lying in, in order that she should be in the neighbourhood of the Lying In Hospital at Lambeth, where she had a letter of admission as soon as she should be in labour, that she was accordingly admitted into the licensed hospital for Lying In Women in the said parish of St Mary Lambeth in which hospital on the fourth day of this instant she was delivered of a male bastard child which has not yet been baptised, and which child is now living.

18 Sept 1790

LMA P85/MRY/1/232

Harriet Lane, "the wife of William Lane of no. 38 Marshal Street, London Road who is a native of the island of Barbadoes in the West Indies and has never gained a settlement in this country.
Not taken in consequence of H Lane being a black woman and not knowing the nature of an oath"

6 Mar 1822[33]

LMA H1/GLI/B11/9

---

[33] The examination is not dated, but its location in the larger sequence suggests the year was 1822.

3   Theatre Play bills

Lambeth first developed its reputation as a metropolitan place of entertainment in the 1660's when the riverside pleasure gardens at Vauxhall opened. First called New Spring Gardens and subsequently known simply as Vauxhall Gardens, its location right on the river meant that it was an accessible venue for Londoners who first came by boat to walk in the grounds, eat, drink, dance and listen to the orchestra. It's popularity increased in the late eighteenth century with the construction of the bridges that gave easier road access from Westminster. By the beginning of the nineteenth century Lambeth was an entertainment centre in its own right with a number of important theatres catering for Londoners and increasingly for its own working class and lower middle class audiences. Astley's Amphitheatre on Westminster Bridge Road and the Surrey Theatre on Blackfriars Road both developed originally as circuses in the 1780s but by the 1820s had reinvented themselves as theatres. The Royal Coburg Theatre (subsequently the Victoria Theatre and latterly the Old Vic) opened in 1816. The smaller and cheaper Bower Theatre on Stangate was established in 1838; it described itself as "the only theatre for the working classes".

The heyday of the "transpontine" Lambeth theatres was brief. Vauxhall Gardens closed in 1859. Between 1877 and 1893 the Bower was converted to a warehouse, the Victoria became a temperance coffee house and Astley's was closed down under fire regulations. From the 1860s local working class audiences increasingly favoured the entertainment provided by the new music halls like the Canterbury, Gatti's, the Camberwell Palace and the Metropole. It was only in 1915 that the Old Vic, as it had now become known, reopened as a theatre with the worthy intention of providing high quality productions of Shakespeare for local people. But by this time the respectable middle classes had migrated south to the new suburban theatres that had opened in Kennington, Brixton and Streatham Hill.

The Lambeth theatres of the early nineteenth century were restricted as to what they could perform. Before 1843 it was illegal for these "minor" theatres to present "legitimate" drama - generally defined as comedy, tragedy and farce. This remained the preserve of the West End "patent" theatres in Drury Lane and Covent Garden. Technically a minor theatre like the Surrey could have been prosecuted for staging a Shakespeare play; to avoid this if *Macbeth* or *Hamlet* were to be staged the manager would insert a ballet into the middle of the performance.[34] What started as a ruse to avoid prosecution ended up by defining the peculiar amalgam that was South London theatre. It was one that combined many different genres of entertainment: circus, pantomime, melodrama, songs, historical pageant, *entr'acte* acrobatics and military spectacle - often all in the same evening's performance. As one West End critic, describing a performance at the Surrey commented, *A minor theatre is the proper region of melodrame - an entertainment to which we have no objection provided it be found in its right place* .[35]

The collection of playbills at Lambeth Archives document the performances at these local theatres for the period 1815 - 1870. They are a much consulted source for traditional theatre history and provide a great deal of detail about the venues, the performers and the types of shows that were staged. Much of the performance that took place - particularly the equestrian drama, spectacles, singers and acrobats - was fugitive in the sense that it was never scripted or published; and the playbills often provide the only record. These playbills had not previously been looked at systematically for the evidence they contain that might relate to black history. A few highlights of black performers in Lambeth were already well known: the black American classical actor Ira Aldridge who gave his first English performances at the Surrey and Royal Coburg theatres in the early 1820's; the famous dancer William Henry Lane, who appeared under his stage name Master Juba and was a big success at Vauxhall Gardens and the Surrey in the late 1840's; and Paul Robeson who starred at the Streatham Hill Theatre in the 1930's. It seemed likely that a detailed study of the collections would provide further evidence.

Our first assumption was that we might simply find evidence of a few local black performers. In fact the evidence of the theatre collections proved to be more complex than that. In addition to playbills that described performances by named black actors, musicians, singers and acrobats we also found a considerable body of plays and other performances whose themes or plots were about some aspect of black or colonial history. We also found a lot of evidence of the developing taste among white performers for "black-face" acts, appearing as "Ethiopians" and "Nigger minstrels".

---

[34] For example "the dramatic and pantomime scene of Othello, the moor of Venice", Vauxhall Gardens playbill, 15 June 1846

[35] George Daniel, "Remarks on *The Inchcape Bell*". London n.d [1828]

40

Theatre was one of the most effective methods of mass-communication to a pre-literate nineteenth century audience. It is difficult to assess just how influential it was. But one anecdote is telling for what it suggests about the power of theatrical performances to shape attitudes. A negro beggar who did casual work as a porter in the London meat markets told Henry Mayhew, *The butchers call me Othello, and ask me why I killed my wife.* [36] The large number of plays with a black or colonial theme showing in Lambeth is therefore interesting because of the way it must have informed contemporary attitudes to black people as well as the awareness of issues like slavery and colonial conquest.

Many of the plays with an ostensibly black or Asian title - *Albamar The Moor*, *Blue Beard and the Flying Indian*, *The Story of Sultan Mowrad and his Welcome Guest* - were clearly little more than fairy tale plots that used foreign characters and exotic locations and probably worked in an established pantomime tradition. [37] But there was also a large number of plays inspired by the contemporary debate about slavery. There was an existing tradition of slave drama in eighteenth century London theatre. Aphra Behn's seventeenth century novel of slavery *Oronooko* had been adapted for both stage and opera as *The Slave* or *The Revolt of Surinam*. Indeed when David Garrick chose to revive the play at Covent Garden in the 1780s it was specifically for its anti-slavery message that he passionately supported. Other Covent Garden performances included *Inkle and Yarico* and *The Blackamoor Wash'd White*. These were in the same tradition and confirmed London audiences' growing familiarity with black people and black issues.

The new South London theatres seem to have quickly developed their own versions of "slave plantation melodrama". Ira Aldridge, the black American actor, made his first appearance in this country as Oronooko in *The Revolt of Surinam* at the Royal Coburg Theatre in 1825. [38] Aldridge's performance is famous for being that of the first classical black actor in England, but this overlooks the fact that this was just one of a number of locally staged performances on the same theme, albeit that the others were performed by white actors. There are many less famous pieces where, in some instances, the texts do not survive. Plays like *Agamemnon the Faithful Negro*, *Black Caesar* (Pl. 11), *The Negro's Hate*, and *My Poll and my Partner Joe* were all

---

[36] Henry Mayhew, *London Labour and the London Poor*, vol.IV, p 426

[37] *Albamar*....Surrey Theatre, 9 Apr. 1849; *Blue Beard*....Astley's Amphitheatre, 2 Sept. 1828; *Sultan Mowrad*....Canterbury Theatre, [1858].

[38] Peter Fryer, *Staying Power*, p253

performed in Lambeth theatres between 1820 and 1835.[39] In the absence of surviving play scripts for many of these performances, the cast lists and extended descriptions of scenes given in the playbills allow us to reconstruct some sense of the plot.

These plays developed out of the traditional "Gothic" melodrama of the London stage with its wild landscapes, historical settings, fanciful architecture and familiar character stereotypes - hero, heroine, villain, buffoon, good old man etc.. Rewritten as slave drama they provided a sharply polarised presentation of the issues. Against the backdrop of a Caribbean or American slave plantation would be found a figure of evil (often the plantation overseer), the innately good but perhaps initially misguided young male lead (often the heir to the plantation), the love interest (who might be white, mulatto or black) and the black lead who often seemed to conform to one of two possible archetypes: the faithful *Uncle Tom* or the angry, revolutionary *Dred* figure. The dramatic tradition of the melodrama would not have allowed the actors any very subtle depiction of these characters. The requirements were for extravagant gestures, movements and facial expression coupled with rhetorical and highly emotional speech.

While such plays contributed to or at least reflected the contemporary debate about slavery, it is doubtful if they did much more than reinforce certain widely held national assumptions. There was a great deal of interest, if not occasionally complacency, about the topic. England had been the first major European power to abolish first the slave trade in 1807 and then slavery itself in 1833. It was also most vigorous in enforcing these changes to international law on other less enthusiastic nations. Yet England's transition from major player in the slave trade at the end of the eighteenth century to leader of the abolitionist movement by the beginning of the nineteenth had been an uncomfortably rapid one. A slightly smug nationalism was one result of this speedy occupation of the moral high ground; and this seems to have influenced the rather sentimental plotting of these slave dramas. One at least appears to distinguish between the behaviour of British, French and Dutch plantation owners.[40]

The first phase of slave dramas in Lambeth theatres was performed in the 1820s and early 1830s. Presumably the abolition of slavery by parliament in 1833 meant that it was no longer the campaigning issue it had been and local theatres then seemed to

---

[39] *Agamemnon,* Astley's Amphitheatre, 17 June 1824; *Black Caesar,* Surrey Theatre, 11 June 1825; *Negro's Hate,* Astley's Amphitheatre, 11 June 1829; *My Poll...,* Surrey Theatre, 9 Nov. 1835.

[40] *Agamemnon The Faithful Negro*, Astley's Amphitheatre, 17 June 1824

have dropped it as a subject. However slavery persisted elsewhere in Brazil, Cuba and most uneasily for an English audience, in the Southern States of the USA. The abolitionist movement in the USA peaked in the 1850s and the effectiveness of its message was clearly heard in Lambeth. *Uncle Tom's Cabin*, published in 1852, was the best-seller of the decade as both a novel and as a drama. There were at least nine different stage versions of the book and four of them were playing Lambeth theatres at the end of 1852 including, rather improbably, an equestrian version of the story at Astley's. Harriet Beecher Stowe's second slavery novel *Dred* was also dramatised and ran at at least two Lambeth theatres in 1856.[41] The renewed interest in the slavery question during the American Civil War in the 1850s and 1860s seems to have prompted local revivals of plays such as *Black Caesar* and *Slave or The Revolt of Surinam* that had first been staged in Lambeth in the 1820s.[42] When the Surrey revived *My Poll and My Partner Joe* in 1850 the playbill suggests that it had been significantly rewritten to incorporate a contemporary slave angle and a local Battersea setting. The original play had been a nautical melodrama involving pirates. The 1850 version seems to replace these with acts set between decks on a slave ship involving Zinga a negro and Zamba a negress. [43]

The Bower Saloon revived *Obi or Three-Fingered Jack* twice in 1858 and 1862 and staged one of its famous trained-dog dramas *The Africans Revenge or Dogs of the Plantation* in the same year.[44] *Obi* had first been performed at the Haymarket Theatre in 1800. It was a melodrama set in the West Indies with the black slaves Tuckey, Quashee and Sam providing the comic relief. It nevertheless contained lines that must have acquired a particular resonance over sixty years. As Quashee says

---

[41] *Uncle Tom's Cabin* played at The Bower during the summer of 1852 "for upwards of 200 nights"; it was staged at The Surrey in November and December 1852 for nine weeks. In the same month at Astley's Amphitheatre "Mr Batty respectfully announces that, in compliance with numerous suggestions and requests, he has determined upon the production of an Equestrian version of Uncle Tom's Cabin embodying all the stirring situations so graphically described in Mrs. Harriet Beecher Stowe's popular work." The play was revived at the Victoria Palace in October 1858, having presumably played there earlier in the decade. It continued to be revived regularly at South London Theatres into the 1890s. *Dred* played at the Surrey Theatre in Dec. 1856 and at The Canterbury

[42] *Slave,* Surrey Theatre, 15 July 1850 and Bower Saloon, 27 July 1861; *Black Caesar,* Bower Saloon, 17 Jan. 1861

[43] *My Poll and My Partner Joe,* Surrey Theatre playbills, 9 November 1835 & 3 June 1850. See *The Revels History of Drama in English,* Vol. VI, p 225 for an account of the 1835 version.

[44] *The African's Revenge or Dogs of the Plantation,* Bower Saloon, [1862]. There was a fashion for dramas involving trained dogs and this is one of many such staged at the Bower in the 1860s that involved dogs in the plot. They were trained to jump at the throat of the villain who was suitably protected with a red cloth

Ah we poor blacks have a weary time of it, and are as much railed at as if the darkness of our skins were a sample of the colour of our hearts.

But this is ultimately sentimental melodrama; and at the conclusion of the play Ormerond, the wicked plantation owner frees his slaves. One can only guess at the extent to which a Lambeth theatre audience in 1862, perhaps familiar with the arguments of the American abolitionists and the causes of the Civil War, would have appreciated the dramatic irony. [45]

The slave plantation melodrama might have become a staple of the Lambeth stage in these years. But the play bills also record a significant number of other plays set in London, France and the USA that featured black characters in other settings. The Bower Saloon revived *The Black Doctor*, a French melodrama whose hero was a negro physician. This had been first performed in London by Ira Aldridge in 1846, but the Bower performance was almost certainly by a white actor. [46] Most of the other parts in plays are minor ones - servants, slaves or street musicians - but they are nevertheless significant in reminding us that black people were an integral part of the fabric of white urban society that theatre audiences were already familiar with. When Pierce Egan's low-life tales, *Life in London,* was first dramatised as *Tom and Jerry* at the Adelphi in 1828, the author wrote in a bit part for Billy Waters, a well known one legged negro violinist who had a pitch outside the theatre. Characters like Jupiter and Audrobal in *Curse of Mammon,* Black Sall in *Scenes from Tom and Jerry* and "Banjo Bill, the leader of the nigger band" in *How We Live in London* were clearly stock characters, perhaps even becoming something of a dramatic cliché by the 1860s (see Pl. 16). [47]

However the English found no contradiction between their role as friend of liberty and supporter of the freed slave and that of colonial conqueror. If melodrama with its sentimental plotting and extremes of emotion lent itself to dramatisations of slavery, another dramatic staple of the Lambeth theatres, the equestrian spectacle - developed initially at Astley's Amphitheatre with its circus traditions - was equally well suited to celebrations of British military prowess. And in the nineteenth century apart from the

---

[45] *Obi or Three-Fingered Jack*, Bower Saloon, August 1858; *Three-Fingered Jack or Death Kaffo,* Bower Saloon Nov.1862. The latter appears to be an adaptation of the former and has acquired a tiger in the cast! For the 1800 Haymarket production see *The Revels History of Drama in English,* Vol. VI, pp 204-5

[46] *The Black Doctor or The Fatal Lover,* Bower Saloon, 3 Aug 1861; for a description of the play see *The Revels History of Drama in English,* Vol. VI, p 237.

endless re-enactments of the Battle of Waterloo and the Crimean war campaigns this meant depictions of the various contemporary wars of colonial conquest in India, Burma, China, Algeria, Ethiopia, South Africa and elsewhere that presented a quite different take on black and Asian people. Such spectacular and triumphalist re-enactments of recent military events were shown in many theatres throughout the nineteenth century. In Lambeth performances such as *The Bombardment of Algiers*, *The Storming of Seringapatam*, *The Relief of Lucknow* and *The Conquest of Magdala* (Pl. 17 & 18) worked on a number of levels. [48] They were spectacular pieces of entertainment with the stage full of horses, military uniforms and fireworks simulating explosions and gun fire. They provided a highly visual, simplified and nationalist interpretation of world affairs for local audiences. They were frequently staged within weeks or months of the actual military event and may even have functioned as a kind of news summary for the less literate in the audience.[49] Inevitably they also served to reinforce assumptions about the desirability and inevitability of European imperialism while portraying black and Asian people as militarily, technologically and, by extension, culturally inferior.

To take one example, the various colonial assaults on the North African city of Algiers by the British and the French were a recurring subject for local theatres. The bombardment by the British navy was "celebrated" in *Slaves of Barbary or British Vengeance* at the Surrey in 1816 *with a grand concluding view of the town, citadel shipping and bombardment of Algiers*. It was also re-enacted at the Lion Pleasure Grounds. In 1828 at Vauxhall Gardens there was a display of *a real Congreve war rocket as used in the bombardment of Algiers and other fortified towns and recently in the attacks on Rangoon against the Burmese…….. The dreadful machine will be securely bound to a large stake, driven into the earth and thus ignited will show the intensity of its powers of burning*. In 1836 at the Surrey Theatre the events were dramatised as melodrama in *Barbarossa or the Tyrant of Algiers*. Later French incursions were also turned into theatre. It was presented as melodrama at the Surrey as *Lily of the Desert and the Arab Spy*. The later French victory, *The Battle of Constantine* was re-enacted at Astley's which, the local press noted, *enables Mr. Cook to bring upon the stage, with brilliant effect, his magnificent stud of trained horses, as*

[47] *Scenes from Tom and Jerry,* Bower Saloon, May 1861; *Curse of Mammon,* Surrey Theatre, April 1859; *How we Live in London,* Surrey Theatre, March 1856
[48] Lion Pleasure Gardens playbill, n.d.; Astleys Amphitheatre playbill, April 1829; Bower Saloon playbill, n.d.[ca. 1861]; Astley's Amphitheatre playbill, Sept 1868
[49] The battle of the Alma in the Crimean War took place on 20 September 1854. By 26 Dec 1854 Astley's Amphitheatre had re-enacted it 55 times!

well as the entire resources of his vast establishment.[50] By complete contrast, a generation after the British bombardment, the inhabitants of Algiers were sufficiently rehabilitated for *The Algerine Family* to appear at Vauxhall in 1851; an act *whose recent arrival in this country has excited so much curiosity.......It is believed this is the first appearance of Mohammedan females in England.*[51]

These slave melodrama and colonial spectacles show that there were many performances which required actors to play black and Asian characters. But the evidence is that almost all of the actors were white. There were black performers in Lambeth in the early nineteenth century, but classical actors like Ira Aldridge were very much the exception. The situation had changed a little by the 1860s when it was recognised that American black actors could and would perform in London rather than the USA where their presence was not encouraged. The *South London Press* reported the instance of Morgan Smith,

a negro actor of Philadelphia ......whose colour has been a bar to his appearing in any theatre in his own country is about to appear on the English stage.[52]

The earliest identified black entertainer in Lambeth seems to have been a trick horse rider who appeared at Astley's Amphitheatre in 1824 where among

a numerous train of Voltigeurs [acrobats]*, among whom will appear Mr O'Donnel, being his first appearance at the Amphitheatre. The African Youth will go through some difficult vaulting exercises on the hunting mare of Arabian breed, Zemira.*[53]

Many such acts presented the race of the performer as part of the attraction. The Ioway Indians, Algerian horseriders, Aboriginal rope-walkers, Bedouin gymnasts, Indian jugglers, animal tamers and dwarves who appeared at Astley's, The Bower and Vauxhall Gardens in the 1840s and 1850s were billed as clever anthropological curiosities, at one remove from that of the circus "freak show". One such was Mohammed Ben Al Hagghe who appeared at Vauxhall described as

[50] *Slaves in Barbary*, Surrey Theatre, 16 Aug. 1816; *Congreve Rocket,* Vauxhall Pleasure Gardens, 18 June 1828; *Barbarossa,* Surrey Theatre, 1836; *Lily of the Desert,* Surrey Theatre, 28 May 1849; *Battle of Constantine,* Astley's Amphitheatre, 13 Apr. 1857 & *South London Journal,* 21 April 1857
[51] Surrey Theatre playbill, 26 Feb 1836; Vauxhall Pleasure Gardens playbill, 18 June 1851
[52] *South London Press*, 7 July 1866
[53] Astley's Amphitheatre playbill, 11 June 1825.

the greatest vaulter in the world. Throwing somersaults over 18 men, with drawn swords uplifted in the air, and leaping as a lion or tiger…. A native of Agra displaying the modes of attack and defence of the Sikhs, and other actions of India. [54]

The theatre career of an African princess trying to make a living in Lambeth in 1886 was similarly restricted. Princess Azahmglona was the niece of the Zulu King, Cetewayo. After his capture in South Africa she had come to Britain and together with 'others of her own race' had arranged to give certain entertainments and war dances. She joined a troupe performing *Uncle Tom's Cabin* in London but she was left destitute due to cancellation by the agent. She was then engaged to perform at the Royal Victoria Hall, Waterloo Road, presumably performing more war dances. [55]

The most successful early black performer - and one of the first to be recognised for his skill at what he did rather than just for being black - was William Henry Lane who appeared under his stage name, Master Juba. [56] He was the headline attraction at Vauxhall Gardens season in 1848 (Pl. 12 & 13) and repeated his success at the Surrey Theatre in the following summer. He was helped by a very favourable review of his act by Charles Dickens who had seen him six years earlier in New York. Like Aldridge fifteen years earlier, Master Juba had to work with the very double-edged notoriety of being the first black performer in his field. In the words of the Vauxhall Garden's playbill announcing his first performance, he was *the only youth of colour that has visited England for the purpose of delineating Negro life and character.* [57] Lane's London career was brief but spectacular. He was the darling of the press for a couple of seasons and is then supposed to have died in London from exhaustion in 1852.

Master Juba's act was an early example of what was to become known as a "Nigger minstrel " show. Such acts were becoming a regular feature of the London and Lambeth stage by the 1840s. The earliest Lambeth example may have been Mr Widdicomb Jnr. singing 'Lubbly Rosa! Sambo come home' at Astley's in 1836. [58] Many such acts initially described themselves as "Ethiopian" - suggesting an exotic and slightly indeterminate African-ness (See Pl. 14). However the tradition, if not the actual performers, was clearly Afro-American. These acts became particularly popular

---

[54] Vauxhall Gardens playbill, 1849
[55] *Westminster and Lambeth Gazette*, 15 May 1886
[56] The name Juba may have been derived from Maria Edgworth's novel, *Belinda,* published in 1802 in which the black servant is called Juba
[57] Vauxhall Gardens playbill, 12 June 1848.
[58] Astleys Amphitheatre playbill, 26 Oct. 1836.

in the 1860s when the American Civil War highlighted the plight of the still-enslaved blacks in the South. Often it was difficult to distinguish whether the performers were black or "black face". Certainly Mr Widdicomb and most of the earlier acts were white. The American Southern Minstrels, who appeared at Vauxhall in 1844, described their act as *the sports and pastimes of the American coloured race.... altogether free from any objectionable feature* - which presumably meant that they were "free" of "objectionable" black performers as well.[59] A typical act from the 1860s was the Savannah Minstrels who appeared at the Bower Saloon several times (Pl. 19): *the best, most refined and mirth-creating entertainers .... comprising songs, duets, glees, refined Negro dances.* Yet it was never clear whether Messrs Wallace, Hankeyson, Talbot, Edmonds, King and Hollingsworth, together with "Washington Selby, the American prize jig dancer" were the real thing, nor indeed quite what the real thing for a Lambeth audience would have been.[60] Another performer at the Bower in the previous month, "Mr Lawrence in his Nigger entertainment", was almost certainly a white singer.[61] However when Ira Aldridge reappeared on the London stage as Othello in 1865, he was described in *the South London Press* as "this real black".[62]

It is clear from press reporting that these "Nigger" minstrel acts were widely enjoyed. They featured regularly at Lambeth theatres and music halls. Some of the performers were indeed black (See Pl. 15). Messrs Smith and Wilson, described as 'sensation Blacks' and 'two darkies full of humour", were performing at Gatti's Music Hall in Westminster Bridge Road in 1866.[63] But it is interesting that similar minstrel acts were just as popular at the rather more genteel Clapham Hall where the CCC Amateur Negro Minstrels, the Royal Christie Original Minstrels and the Royal Aboriginal Minstrels all performed in the late 1860's and were all probably "black face" acts.[64] The Clapham Hall also hosted several more serious events about the genre, with discussions as to the relative merits of white and black minstrels and a lecture on "nigger minstrelsy". Among the performers mentioned are Jim Crow, the "Ethiopian Serenaders", Banjo, Bones and Co. and Sam Blank all of whom were apparently white but dressed to look black.[65]

---

[59] Vauxhall Gardens playbill, 30 Sept 1844.
[60] Bower Saloon playbill, 16 Sept 1861.
[61] Bower Saloon playbill, 26 Aug 1861.
[62] *South London Press*, 26 Aug 1865
[63] *South London Press*, 13 Jan 1866
[64] *Clapham Gazette & Local Advertiser*, 1 Feb 1869, 1 July 1869, 1 Dec 1870
[65] *Clapham Gazette & Local Advertiser*, 1 June 1861 and 1 Feb 1868

In the late 1860's the popular interest in minstrel shows was expanded by visits from black American touring choirs singing gospel songs. Unlike minstrel shows that were unashamedly populist in their appeal, these choirs were presented much more seriously. They performed mainly in churches and public halls rather than theatres. Most were composed of recently freed slaves and their tours of England were frequently linked to both fund raising and consciousness raising. Many enjoyed royal and aristocratic patronage. The Fisk Jubilee singers (See front cover) who performed an evening of sacred songs at the George Street Mission in Lambeth Walk in 1888 were raising funds for the Fisk University, Tennessee, one of the first black universities in America. Mr Hutchinson of Brixton who introduced the singers urged *all present to use their personal influence in doing what they could to aid their coloured brethren in distant lands*. The previous year the Pennsylvania Jubilee singers had appeared at Christ Church Lambeth where they reportedly *gave some excellent selections*.[66]

The evidence assembled here is arbitrary in the sense that the theatre collections and newspapers looked at are by no means complete. As has already been suggested there remains a considerable amount of work to be done in this field. Nevertheless the material that has been found is sufficient to demonstrate that there was a significant black presence in the theatres of South London in the nineteenth century. Not only were individual black performers important attractions for white audiences but, more persuasively, these same audiences were presented with regular portrayals of black people, albeit frequently caricatured or melodramatic, which nevertheless grew in stature through the century. In particular the slavery melodramas and the touring black gospel choirs must have been, in their different ways, instrumental in shaping and changing attitudes to black people.

---

[66] *Westminster & Lambeth Gazette,* 14 May 1887 and 10 Nov 1888

Lambeth Theatre playbills

Astley's Amphitheatre   1820-1868

Xaia of China or The Fatal Flood gate	3 Apr, 15 May 1820	12/951
Veiled Prophet of Khorashan	10 July 1820	12/951
Lala Rooke	15, 21, 28 Aug 1820	12/951
Yarra or The Indian rivals	28 & 31 Oct 1820	12/951
Agamemnon the Faithful Negro; slave plantation melodrama with British, French and Dutch planters. Includes "a new Cocoa Nut dance"	17 & 21 Jun 1824	12/951
Death of the Moor defending his Flag	27 Sept 1824	12/951
Gymnasia "By a numerous train of Voltigeurs, among whom will appear Mr O'Donnel, being his first appearance at the Amphitheatre. The African Youth will go through some difficult vaulting exercises on the hunting mare of Arabian breed, Zemira"	18 Jul 1825	12/951
Death of the Moor defending his Flag "in which Mr Ducrow will make use of a scimitar that was made a present to him together with twelve tiger skins by the Persian ambassador"	11 Oct 1825	12/951
Burmese War! or , Our Victories in the East. with Two Wild Coursers, In the Scene of the Indian Hunter! Clowns to the Circle, Messrs, Buccley, & J. Ducrow	3 Apr, 8, 15 May 1826	LAD
Three Sultanas.	1826	LAD
War In India; or, the Burmese Empire.	May, Jun, Jul 1826.	LAD
The British Artist or The Hundred Arabian Steeds. 100 Horses. with Athletic Matches by 60 Wrestlers and Warriors, Arabs exercising their Steeds for the prize Dgerid with The Wild Horse, The Horse Aboukir, The High Trained Charger, & The Negro's Pony.	11Jun 1827	LAD
Surprising feats on the elastic cord by the Flying Indian. with Battle of Navarino or The Arab of the Desert.	Jun1828.	LAD
Blue Beard and the Flying Indian	2 Sep 1828	LAD
Storming Of Seringapatam or the death of Tippoo-saib.	April 1829.	LAD

Cataract of the Ganges with The splendid Procession of the Rajah's Cortege. with Negro's Hate; plantation melodrama	31 Aug 1829	LAD
Horse Banditti on their 40 steeds	nd	LAD
Arab of the Red Desert	nd	LAD
Grand Pyramids of men and horses! From the celebrated piece of the Elephant Of Siam!	25 Sept. 1830.	LAD
Wild Zebra Hunt; introduction of Nallas, Female Slaves. with Yellala, the Wild Zebra by the Sultan to the Queen, in a brilliant Parmeliox, formed of pyrotechnical fountains of real fire. Hatman Danfodio, Sultan of Fellatah, Mr Ducrow.	1 October 1832.	LAD
Second representation of a new gymnastic scene on a single horse, by eight equestrians, called, the Catawha Indians,	18th June 1833.	LAD
The four quarters of the globe! Europe, with her white palfrey,---Asia, with her state charger, Africa, in her car drawn by pigmy elephants!	Sept & Oct 1833.	LAD
Introduction of the Arab And Bedouin gymnastic feats!	n.d. [1836]	LAD
Grand Arabian Spectacle !! 100 Bare Steeds! or the Enchanted Arabs!! Including Indian ballad singers. with Lalla Rookh or Ghebeols of the Desert! including Jumbo and Sambo (Two Blacks) played by Messrs Widdicomb Jnr and J. George with contest of drowning steeds. – Indian war boats. [engraved illustration]	14 Jul, Aug, 15 Sept 1836.	LAD
Mr Widdicomb Jnr will sing 'Lubbly Rosa! Sambo come home'	7 Oct 1836.	LAD
Arab and Bedouin gymnastic feats.	16 May 1838.	LAD
Indian Hunting Girl.	28 May,11 Sept, 7 Oct 1838.	LAD
Mr Mosley, will for the first time, execute his brilliant scene of the 'Wild Indian of the Prairie'	14 Mar 1842.	LAD
Morocco Arabs.	25Sept 1843.	LAD
Bride of the Nile.	15 Sept, 6 Oct 1845.	LAD
Forty Thieves! Or Harlequin Ali Baba and the robbers cave.	11 Jan1847.	LAD
Surrender of the Amazons; approach to the city of Granada; Amazonian cavalry and their Andulusian steeds! General conflict of the forces; triumph of Ismael and Zulma – and the last grand tableau.	13, 20 Mar 1848.	LAD

Morok the Beast Tamer. Part 2 India 1875.	24 Apr 1848	LAD
Amazonian Maids and their war steeds.	4 Jun 1849 24Nov1851.	LAD
The Victim Cast into the Nile; Act 3. the Mighty Desert! the Dream Spirit, Nocturnal Visions of the Desert.	1 Dec 1851.	LAD
Part of the menagerie of the Sultan.	1 Nov.1852	LAD
Return of the Sultan from the 'Ahairea' or 'Spring Hunt' - attended by his officers and mounted huntsmen, slaves, sacred standard bearers and real elephants. with Uncle Tom's Cabin "Mr Batty respectfully announces that, in compliance with numerous suggestions and requests, he has determined upon the production of an Equestrian version of Uncle Tom's Cabin embodying all the stirring situations so graphically described in Mrs. Harriet Beecher Stowe's popular work and which are particularly adapted to the resources of this Theatre"	8, 15 Nov 1852	LAD
"Mr W Harlow will appear in a pantomimical delineation as The Slave! Or Terrors of the Lash."	18 June 1853	LAD
The Bombardment and capture of Canton... "Victory! The British and French flags wave triumphantly upon the walls of Canton"	n.d. [post 1855]	LAD
French in Algiers or The Battle of Constantine.... "Total defeat of the Kabyles! Victory of la Belle France"	13 Apr 1857	LAD
Jibbenainosay or The White Horse of Nick of the woods US colonial drama with settlers "Ralph Stackpole, a subject for lynch law, Emperor, a Negro and the Shawnee Indians	1 Mar 1858	LAD
Revolt in the East or The Fugitives and their faithful steed The retaking of Delhi including "the burning of the factories......destruction of the arsenal and defeat of the mutinous Sepoys....the Indians at bay	13 Dec 1858	LAD
Conquest of Magdala or, The War in Abyssinia	1868	LAD
The Conquest of Magdala and the fall of Theodore; dramatisation of British invasion of Abyssinia under Sir Robert Napier[67]	Sept 12 1868	LAD
Ravine & Cataract of the great Miami. The Lovers-The Ford-Attack of the Shawnees.	n.d.	LAD
Madame Howard, The African Lion Faced Lady, is paying a short visit to this town. This Wonderful Freak of Nature Must be seen to be believed.	October 1883.	12/951 cuttings

---

[67] The British capture of Magdala and the suicide of the Emperor Theodore took place during April 1868

The Bower Saloon   1846 - 62

The Ioway Indians "in their native costume will go through the whole of their evolutions concluding with their peculiar manner of warfare, also the dance called the Death Dance"	Jul 16 1846	12/951 S5061
Orson The Wild Man of the Wood	n.d	12/951 S5061
Ali Pacha or The Tyrant of Aleppo	n.d.	12/951 S5061
Jocko or The Ape of Brazil; featuring Sig. Martini, the man monkey	n.d	12/951 S5061
Uncle Tom's Cabin "the heart appalling drama of intense interest.....as played by [Mr T E Mills] upwards of 200 nights"	Aug 9 1852	12/951 S5061
Uncle Tom's Cabin "as played by [Mr T E Mills] upwards of 200 nights"	1852	12/951 S5061
Monkey of the Storm (The Island Ape)	n.d	12/951 S5061
Three Fingered Jack ; slave plantation melodrama	18 Aug 1858	12/951 S5061
Obi _or Three Fingered Jack; slave plantation melodrama	21 Aug 1858	12/951. S5061
Life in the Bush or The Chief of the Broken Bay Tribe Australian colonial melodrama "Chief of the Broken Bay tribe and his followers - let them beware the Caffres just revenge - woe to the Pale face warriors - the chief and his sister - his oath of revenge - now for the White man's stores......."	13 Sept 1858	12/951 S5061
Duke's Fate or The Creole, the Maid and the Student; French melodrama	26 Jan [n.d.]	12/951 S5061
Black Caesar or Jack Union and his Dog Quid A nautical drama[68]	Jan 17 1861	12/951 S5061
"The Greatest Wonders of the Day, The Brothers Pinder including Mr John Pinder "the deaf and dumb artise... (the only living delineation of the peculiarities of the Monkey tribe) as Mushpaug the monkey takes his amusing flights round the gallery" engraved illustration	19 Feb 1861	12/951 S5061
Scenes from Tom and Jerry featuring "Dusty Bob and Black Sall"	8 May 1861	12/951 S5061

---

[68] This is presumably a revival and adaptation - to include a substantial nautical element - of *Black Caesar* performed at the Surrey Theatre on 11 June 1825

Shadow of the Death Torrent or The Emigrant Murderer melodrama set in USA featuring "Pompey White, black help to Silas Ross, a Yankee clockmaker"	20 May 1861	12/951 S5061
Slave or The Revolt of Surinam; cast includes Gambia the slave and Zelinda, mulatto wife to Captain Clifton	22 July 1861	12/951 S5061
Black Doctor or The Fatal Lovers; French melodrama, featuring Fabian a negro doctor and Christian his servant[69]	3 Aug 1861	12/951 S5061
Mr Lawrence "in his nigger entertainment" song The Young Kentuckian	26 Aug 1861	12/951 S5061
The Savannah Minstrels "seven first class singers, musicians and comedians who are pronounced by the entire London press to be the best, most refined and mirth creating entertainers who have appeared in the metropolis. The entertainment is of a refined yet racy character and entirely different to any which has preceded it comprising songs, duets, glees and refined Negro dances, music, vocal and instrumental" [lists performers and song selections, including "The Creole Girl" and "What's dat noise in de Kitchen	16 Sept 1861	12/951 S5061
"The renowned Indian dwarf, Mahomet Baux will appear at the bar"	23 Sept 1861	12/951 S5061
The Celebrated Savannah minstrels "who lately created such a sensation at this theatre will sing their popular song of Old Billy Patterson" with Mahomet Baux, "the only living Indian Chief, the greatest wonder in the world"	28 Sept 1861	12/951 S5061
Mr Alfred Jones, The Savannah Song "with real cocoa nut accompaniment" with The Indian dwarf Mahomet Baux "in his pleasing entertainment of Bob Ridley, Pas Comic, Sailors Hornpipe"	7 Dec 1861	12/951 S5061
The Indian dwarf Mahomet Baux	14 Dec 1861	12/951 S5061
The Indian dwarf Mahomet Baux "who is only 37" high and 23 years of age"	17 Dec 1861	12/951 S5061
Sketches of Indian Life including "The African Pango or long-armed ape", with the relief of Lucknow & the battle of the Amazons	n.d. [post 1861]	12/951 S5061
The Siege of Delhi with Highland Terrier or The Relief of Lucknow	nd [post-1861]	12/951 S5061
"The third appearance of the Indian dwarf Mahomet Baux since his provincial tour"	31 Mar 1862	12/951 S5061

---

[69] This is a revival of the play first performed at the City of London Theatre in 1846 with Ira Aldridge as Fabian, the negro physician

Mahomet Baux The Indian dwarf , "Sailors Hornpipe"	28 Apr, 3 May 1862	12/951 S5061
Three Fingered Jack or The Death Kaffo; plantation set melodrama featuring slaves, planter, overseer and a tiger[70]	22 Nov 1862	12/951 S5061
The Pirate Chief or The Black Flag And the Treacherous Sambo	nd [1862?]	12/951 S5061
The African's Revenge or The Dogs of the Plantation "Death by the fangs of dogs; Mr and Mrs J Emmet and their wonderful dogs"[71] . [Performance of Othello is also on the bill]	n.d. [1862?}	12/951 S5061

The Canterbury Theatre   1858

The Story of the Sultan Mowrad and his Welcome Guest	c. 1858	LAD
songs from Dred	n.d. [1856]	LAD

The Surrey Theatre   1816- 1856

Slaves in Barbary or British Vengeance, with "a grand concluding view of the town, citadel, shipping and bombardment of Algiers" ; dramatisation of British navy attack	16 Aug 1816	3/951 S5060
Columbus	26 Feb 1822	3/951 S5060
Robinson Crusoe	2 May 1822	3/951 S5060
Barber of the Mill of Bagdad	21 Oct 1822	3/951 S5060
Fire Worshippers	28 Apr 1824	3/951 S5060
Abdellac or The Barbary Corsair or The English Fisherman of Algiers; dramatisation of the bombardment of Algiers by the British navy	3 Jan 1825	3/951 S5060

---

[70] A revival and adaptation of *Obi or Three Fingered Jack* performed at the Bower in August 1858

[71] The Bower playbill for 22 March 1862 include an engraving of a black man being attacked by a dog, but does not list this performance. There was a fashion for dramas involving trained dogs and this is one of many such staged at the Bower in the 1860s that involved dogs in the plot. They were trained to jump at the throat of the villain who was suitably protected with a red cloth

Black Caesar or The Fatal Thicket Slave plantation set melodrama; "the piece concludes with an awful feature of retributive vengeance"[72] with Jocko or The Orang Utang of Brazil melodrama set on a Brazilian rice plantation; Mons. Gouffe as the Brazilian Ape will "perform his extraordinary jumps and feats of posturing and conclude… by running round the Auditory upon the half inch beading of the boxes and gallery"	11 Jun 1825	3/951 S5060
Mons. Gouffe in The Island Ape "including his extraordinary leaps, features of agility and gymnastic displays, horizontal balancings, supporting a boy on his shoulders, never attempted by any man but himself to conclude with his running round the fronts of the boxes and gallery supported by the thread-like mouldings"	11 Jun 1825	3/951 S5060
My Poll and my Partner Joe nautical melodrama[73]	9 Nov 1835	3/951 S5060
Barbarossa or the Tyrant of Algiers	22 Feb 1836	3/951 S5060
The Slave! operatic version of The Revolt of Surinam with Bronze Horse, Chinese melodrama	8 Feb 1836	3/951 S5060
"Mr. Webster will sing in character a popular melody from his Lenten entertainment called Jim Crow"	28 Mar 1836	3/951 S5060
The Real Bedouin Arabs, "Hossein, Sidi Ali, Hassan &c. &c."	15 Jul 1839	3/951 S5060
Curse of Mammon; comedy based on Hogarth's Marriage a la Mode featuring Jupiter " a Black" and Audrobal "a negro boy" with The Giant of Palestine, Crusader melodrama	26 Apr 1839	3/951 S5060
Jocko The Brazilian Ape	8 April 1840	3/951 S5060
Governor's Wife, colonial melodrama with Neb "a black"	16 Aug 1847	3/951 S5060
Alhamar the Moor Medieval Spanish melodrama	9 & 16 Apr 1849	3/951 S5060
G W Pell "with his popular and inimitable troupe of vocal and instrumental delineators of negro peculiarities will appear and introduce various novelties, in an Ethiopian concert, aided by the astounding and incredible wonders of the renowned and unapproachable "Juba" whose performances must be witnessed and cannot be described".	23 Apr 1849	3/951 S5060
Lily of the Desert and the Arab Spy Melodrama based on the French conquest of Algiers	28 May 1849	3/951 S5060

---

[72] There is a later revival and adaptation of this play performed at the Bower Saloon on Jan 17 1861

[73] This play was revived and adapted at the Surrey Theatre on 3 June 1850

Wacousta or The Curse; American drama set in Fort Detroit with the Ottowa Indians and Pompey Sip "a coloured gentleman servant in the garrison"	12 Nov 1849	3/951 S5060
G W Pell the original "Bones" and his talented company of Ethiopian Serenaders……"G W Pell will perform on one bone, a la Paganini on one string" lists songs and performers. with Matilda of Lugarto the Mulatto; French melodrama	20 May 1850	3/951 S5060
Matilda of Lugarto the Mulatto; French melodrama with G W Pell's Ethiopian Entertainment, singers accompanied on banjo and bones "to conclude with the celebrated Plantation dance"	20 May 1850	3/951 S5060
G W Pell and his talented company of Ethiopian Serenaders……"will appear and give the following collection of Ethiopian melodies" ; lists songs and performers.	29 May 1850	3/951 S5060
G W Pell and his talented company of Ethiopian Serenaders . with My Poll and My Partner Joe Slave trade melodrama set in Battersea, Portsmouth and between decks of a slave ship with Black Brandon "captain of the slaver", Zinga "a negro" and Zamba "a negress" [74] with Matilda of Lugarto the Mulatto, 18th century French melodrama	3 June 1850	3/951 S5060
Matilda of Lugarto the Mulatto, 18th century French melodrama with "On Friday June 21st, by express command and under the immediate patronage of Jung Bahadoor Koonwur Ranajee, prime minister and commander in chief of Nepal [and his suite]….. who will on this occasion honour the theatre with their presence, a variety of entertainments"	17 June 1850	3/951 S5060
Red Man or The Mariner and His Dogs, Cherokee Indian melodrama	24 Jun 1850	3/951 S5060
Slave or The Revolt of Surinam, slave plantation operatic drama	15 & 18 Jul 1850	3/951 S5060
"The Surrey Nepaulese Ambassador will ascend for the ninth and tenth times in England on the new Locomotive balloon on the back of a real Jerusalem pony. His princely brothers and the well known interpreter from St Paul's will nightly honour the Royal Surrey Theatre with their presence"	22 Aug, 2, 5, 9 & 23 Sept, 3 Oct 1850	3/951 S5060
Exhibition of 1851 and Mathilda or Lugarto the Mulatto	12 May 1851	3/951 S5060
Uncle Tom's Cabin "Immense hit - triumphant career - ninth week of Surrey Uncle Tom's Cabin"	1 Nov - 27 Dec 1852	3/951 S5060

---

[74] This play was previously performed at the Surrey Theatre on 9 Nov 1835

Oceola! melodrama set in Florida plantation during the Seminole Indian wars. Includes "Yellow Jake the quadroon woodsman and Black Jake the Ebony coachman......both were different coloured slaves on the Randolph's plantation and rivals for the hand of Viola, the beautiful quadroon"	9 May 1853	3/951 S5060
How We Live in London; the cast of "London street folk" include "Banjo Bill, the leader of the nigger band", with Violin, Bones, Tambourine and Beery and a Hindoo tract seller	31 Mar 1856	3/951 S5060
Dred!	1 Dec 1856	3/951 S5060

Vauxhall Gardens   1822- 54

Ramo Samee, The Wonderful Indian Juggler	12 Aug, 1822, 21 Jul 1823, 5, 9 Jul 1828	IV/162/16 / 123, 124, 143, 170, 171
"The novel exhibition in public of a real Congreve War rocket (made for government at the works at Woolwich) As used in the bombardment of Algiers and other fortified towns, and recently on the attacks on Rangoon, etc against the Burmese and the capture of Bhurtpore."[75]	18 June 1828	IV/162/16 / 171 & 14/581 S5060
The Indian Juggler	15 Aug 1830/31	IV/162/ 5/ 3
'Flight of the Arabs' A contest of 8 to 10 horse racers.	13 Aug 1839	IV/162/13/2 21
Evolution's of the Arab Tribe' On 11 fleet steeds, conducted by Signor Hillier. with Ramoo Samee the celebrated Indian, who "will vary his extraordinary juggling performances every night" with Passwan Oglu who "will exhibit his interesting Indian feats in the ballet theatre"	5, 9 Jul 1841	IV/162/13/2 33, 236, 237, 242. IV/162/ 5 / 13
The Wild Evolution's of the Bedouin Tribe or Flight of the Arabs Introducing all the Equestrians with their horses, in corresponding attire.	26, 28, 29, 30 July 1841	IV/162/13/ 258, 268, 270, 272
Amazons (horse racers) by 12 Highly trained Palfreys, mounted by 6 ladies and 6 warriors in rich attire.	2, 4, 6 Aug 1841.	IV/162/13/ 276, 278
'Red Indians' consisting of warriors enlisting, council of war, war dance, and scalping, pipe of peace and Indian wedding.	9, 11 Aug 1841	IV/162/13/ 282 - 288
Passwan Og Lou, Indian Juggler will perform his astonishing feats with balls, knives and daggers.	18 Aug 1841	IV/162/13/ 292

---

[75] The British were fighting in Burma from 1824-1826

Ramoo Samee, Celebrated Indian Juggler	20 Aug 1841	IV/162/13/ 294
Ramoo Samee, Indian juggler	23 Aug 1841	IV/162/13/2 96
Ramoo Samee and Passwan Og Lou; both Indian Jugglers	31 Aug, 1, 2 - 9 Sept 1841.	IV/162/13/ 302 - 308
14 Ioway Indians 'Encampment - 4 wigwams, war and other dances, archery, ball playing and riding.	Sept 1841	IV/162/13/ 407, 408
'War Maids of the Golden Sun' or 'The Amazons and Warriors of the Paly.	29, 30, 31 Aug, 2 Sept. 1842	IV/162/13/ 372, 374, 376, 380
The Fourteen Ioway Indians from near the Rocky mountains, in America; gives names of Indians, with engr. of encampment at Lords cricket ground	9 Sept 1844	IV/162/17/ 34, 35
An Ethiopian Entertainment given by The American Southern Minstrels. "In this entertainment, the sports and pastimes of the American coloured race delineated, (altogether free from any objectionable feature) through the medium of songs, refrains, ditties and dances etc."	30 Sept, 2, 7 Oct 1844	IV/162/13/ 410, 412
'Fancy Fair' The Indian Juggler will perform wonderful events.	4, 11, 12 Aug 1845	IV/162/14/2 6, 27
The dramatic and pantomime scene of Othello, The Moor of Venice.	15–19 Jun 1846	IV/162/14/5 3
The Indian Juggler.	16 July 1845	IV/162/17/ 53
Mons Ferdinand Tournaire "will appear on a steed, without saddle as the Indian juggler."	1 June 1846	IV/162/17/ 59
Horsemanship-The warriors of Ipsara	8˙12 Jun 1846	IV/162/14/ 51
Grand concert- American serenades by the original Creole vocalists.	22 Jun–10 July 1846	IV/162/14/ 55, 57, 59, 61
American serenades by the Creole vocalists.	30Jun- 3 Jul, 6-10 Jul 1846	IV/162/17/ 63, 64
Grand concert – first appearance of Ethiopian harmonist's, songs include 'Somebody in De House' and 'Buffalo Gals'	3 ˙ 14 Aug 1846	IV/162/14 6, /69
Monsieur Ferdinand appears as the Indian Juggler	31Aug – 4 Sept 1846	IV/162/14/7 6
A dramatic equestrian scene of Othello, Moor of Venice played by Mon. Francois Tournaire.	7-11 Sept 1846	IV/162/14

Bedouin Arabs perform before Queen Victoria and Prince Albert and the Prince of Wales.	26 June 1847	IV/162/14/ 99 - 120
Bedouin Arabs, The wonders of the world unrivalled feats of agility and strength.	Jun- Sept 1847	IV/162/17/ 74, 77, 80, 82, 145
The Mexican wonders 'Santa Amesou' and his infant son. (Gymnastic exercises)	9, 10, 16 Aug, 7 Sept 1847.	IV /162/14/ 106, 108, 117
Bedouin Arabs will give unrivalled feats of agility and strength	21 Jun, 12-16, 26 Jul, 9, 10 Aug 1847.	IV/162/14/9 6/ 101/ 102/ 104
The extraordinary performances of the Bedouin Arabs, horsemanship by first rate equestrians.	24Sept 1847	IV/162/14/1 23
A model of the city of Constantinople including the Aurut or Slave market, the beautiful Mosque of Sultan Solomon [etc.]	29 May, 10-13July, 18 Sept 1848	IV/162/14 128, 129, 141, 161
6 Highly talented Ethiopian Serenaders under direction of Mr G.W. Pell (celebrated bone player). with The Inimitable Juba "accomplishes over 200 steps…..the only youth of colour that has visited England for the purpose of delineating Negro life and character." With quotation from Charles Dickens' account of him.	12 Jun1848	IV/162/14/1 32
Ethiopian Olio by the Serenader and Juba.	12 June 1848	IV/162/14/1 33
Six highly–talented Ethiopian serenaders and Juba.	19June 1848	IV/162/14/1 34
Juba and The Grand American Olio! By Pell's Corps of Serenaders.	19 June 1848.	IV/162/17/ 86
Juba the Triumphant and 5 other highly talented Ethiopian Serenaders with Dickens' account	26 June 1848	IV/162/14 136
Grand American Olio featuring Juba "immortalised By 'Boz'" singing "Jenny, put De Kittle on," and the Ethiopian Serenaders.	3, 4 July 1848	IV/162/14/ 139
Dancing by Juba, "A genuine son of the southern clime" [with Charles Dickens' account], Ethiopian Serenaders and Grand American Olio.	July - Aug 1848.	IV/162/14/ 140 - 155
Juba, portrait engr. and review [Illustrated London News?]	5 Aug 1848	IV/162/ 2/12
First appearance in England of Master Juba as "Lucy Long!" In which character he appeared upwards of two hundred nights in the United States.	21 Aug– 18 Sept1848.	IV/162/14 /155 - 161

The Inimitable Juba "who will appear as Lucy Long, and in his much admired Plantation dance."	28 Aug -18 Sept 1848.	IV/162/14/ 156 - 161
The Algerine Family, engr. illustration	1849	IV/162/ 2/12
Mohammed Ben Al Hagghe, "the greatest vaulter in the world. Throwing somersaults over 18 men, with drawn swords uplifted in the air, and leaping as lion, tiger…. Native of Agra displaying the modes of attack and defence of the Sikhs, and other actions of India."	1849	IV/162/ 5/ 17
The Mysterious Zadoc in his Eastern temple.	1849	IV/162/ 5/17
A visit to the Vauxhall Gardens from 'Nepalese Princes' who have honoured the director with their presence on seven different occasions.	July - Aug 1850	IV/162/14/2 15, 219, 233, 237
The Nepaulese Ambassador, his princely brothers, and distinguished suite, who will honour the gardens with their presence for the benefit of the veteran Green	5 July 1850	IV/162/ 5 / 17
The Late Ramoo Samee and his widow to the editor of Bells lLife in London, newspaper article	28 Aug 1850.	IV/162/16 / 121
'The Algerine Family', Whose recent arrival in this country has excited so much curiosity, have been engaged. This interesting groupe consists of the principal, Yousof Ben Ibrahim, three young females of exquisite beauty, wife and sisters of the principal, and a child of uncommon loveliness, aged five years son of Yousoff. It is believed this is the first appearance of Mohammedan females in England; and the interest consequent on the presence of these strangers from an Eastern clime, will be greatly increased by the magnificence, and gorgeousness of their costumes.	May, Jun, Jul, Aug, 8, 9, 15 Sept 1851	IV/162/14/ 248 - 293 & 14/581 S5060
The Algerine Family	31 May 1851	IV/162/5/18
Algerine Family: cutting from Illustrated London News	12 Jul 1851	IV/162/17/ 108
The death of Ramoo Samee- Appeal of the Widow. Ellen Ramoo Samee., newspaper article	21 Aug 1851	IV/162/16/ 123
The Nepaulese Princes	26 Aug 1851	IV/162/ 5 /18
The Hall of Arabs. "has been entirely refitted, and Yousof and his interesting troupe of females, aided by others of his nation, will perform various national dances, songs, customs and ceremonies, exhibiting all the salient peculiarities of the children of the desert."	May-Jun 1852.	IV/162/14/ 303, 305, 311, 313, 327, 329
Hall of Alhambra. Yousof and his interesting group of Arab ladies. National dances, songs, customs and ceremonies.	19, 26 Jul, & Aug 1852	IV/162/14/3 19, 323 - 7
The hall of the Alhambra with the Arab ladies. National dances, songs, customs and ceremonies.	26 July, Aug 1852	IV/162/17/ 112, 115

The Hall of Alhambra with the Arab ladies.	26July 1852	IV/162/14/3 21
Sable Harmonists. "who were received with the greatest enthusiasm on Monday last, in their peculiar and astonishing Ethiopian entertainment."	21, 27 Sept 1852	IV/162/14 / 341
Illustration of Black musicians playing Banjo's and Tambourine.	n.d.	IV/162/17/ 161
The Stupendous Picture, from Drawings furnished from the East India company's Museum [of] The Golden Temple of Guadma and the Great Pagoda of Dagon, Rangoon, Burmese Empire.	30 May, Jun- Aug 1853	IV/162/14 353 - 377
A grand bombardment of the temple of Guadma, Rangoon, will take place.[76]	Jun - Sept 1853, May 1854	IV/162/14/ 357 - 385
Temple of Rangoon, pyrotechnic effects by Madame Cotton	1 Jul 1854	IV 162/ 17/ 117
Storming of the Grand Temple At Rangoon	29 May. Jun-Jul 1854	IV/162/14/ 387 - 405

---

[76] The British captured Rangoon in 1852

Plate 1   Negro's head in Lambeth Palace, ca. 1663

Two wooden life-size portrait busts are the earliest surviving representations of black people in Lambeth. They were carved when the Great Hall was rebuilt between 1660 and 1663. They commemorate the munificence of Archbishop William Juxon who paid for the reconstruction. His family coat of arms consisted of four negro heads; although their significance is unclear.

Plate 2   The Loango Family of Slaves, 1792

This engraving was made by the poet and artist William Blake at his studio in Hercules Buildings in Lambeth. It was one of a series he engraved to illustrate a history of the Negro Rebellion in Surinam written by his friend John Gabriel Stedman. Blake's illustrations show these Africans as the exotic and enslaved inhabitants of a distant Dutch colony. Stedman owned the family; the initials J.G.S are tattooed on the man's breast. But it is clear that Blake would have been as familiar with black people living in Lambeth at the time.

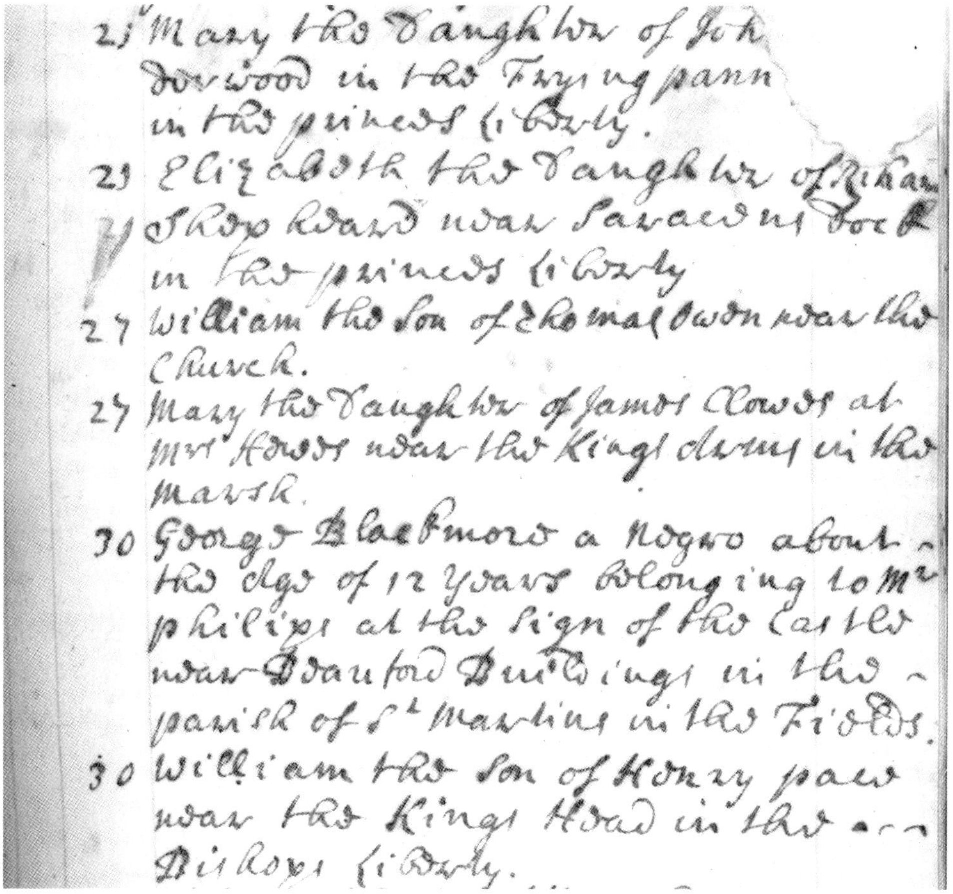

21 Mary the daughter of John Dorwood in the Frying pann in the princes liberty.
21 Elizabeth the daughter of Richard Shepheard near Saracens hed in the princes liberty
27 William the Son of Thomas Owen near the Church.
27 Mary the daughter of James Clowes at Mrs Howes near the Kings Arms in the marsh.
30 George Blackmore a Negro about the age of 12 years belonging to Mr philips at the sign of the Castle near Beaufort Buildings in the parish of St Martins in the Fields.
30 William the Son of Henry paw near the Kings Head in the Bishops liberty.

Plate 3 St. Mary Lambeth Draft Baptism Register, 1702

Because black people were unusual in early eighteenth century Lambeth the baptism register often gave additional information about them. The entry for George Blackmore on the 30 September gives his age, the name and address of his master and, by implication, his trade: "George Blackmore a Negro about the age of 12 years belonging to Mr. Philips at the sign of the Castle near Beaufort Buildings in the parish of St Martins in the Fields".

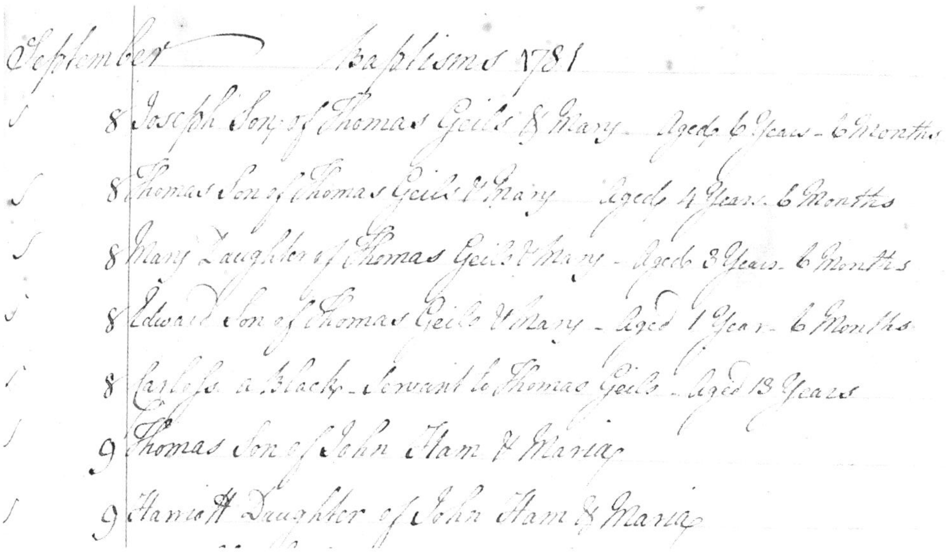

September Baptisms 1781
8 Joseph Son of Thomas Geils & Mary Aged 6 Years 6 Months
8 Thomas Son of Thomas Geils & Mary Aged 4 Years 6 Months
8 Mary Daughter of Thomas Geils & Mary Aged 3 Years 6 Months
8 Edward Son of Thomas Geils & Mary Aged 1 Year 6 Months
8 Carlos a Black Servant to Thomas Geils Aged 13 Years
9 Thomas Son of John Ham & Maria
9 Harriott Daughter of John Ham & Maria

Plate 4 St. Mary Lambeth Baptism Register, 1781

Various elements in the register entry tell us that Carlos, baptised on the 8 September was almost certainly still a slave; his age at baptism, the absence of a surname and the details of his master are all indicators. His position in the register, coming after the four sons and the daughter of his master Thomas Geils who were all baptised on the same day, is equally telling of his servile status.

Baptisms in the Parish of Clapham. 1802

			Baptized	Born
82.	Bannah.	William Bannah, aged 15 years, Son of Naimbanna, the Deputy of Firama King of the Timmaney Country. Africa.	July 31.	
83.	Ka Fodee.	Joseph Williams, aged 15, from Wongapong a town in the Susoo Country. Son of Ka Fodee a Chief in the Rokelle, Africa.	July 31.	
84.	Pa Dick	Peter Smith aged 15, from the Bullam Shore, Son of Pa Dick, & Nephew to Pa Jack, Chief of the Bullam Shore, who visited England in 1794.	July 31.	
85.	Tamba.	William Tamba, aged 12, Son of Pa Tamba a Trader from the Bullam Shore.	July 31.	
86.	Foree Carree	James Fantimanee, aged 10, Son of Foree Carree Trader from the Bullam Shore, now resident at Hakandee, in the Susoo Country.	July 31.	
87.	Hunter	Mary 1st Daughter of Thomas Hunter, & Anne his Wife, late A. Watkis Spr.	Augt 4.	May 10.
88.	Gardener.	Maria 1st Daughter of James Gardener, & Charlotte his Wife, late C. Hodges Spr.	Augt 11.	
89.	Taylor.	Maria 5th Daughter of Wm Taylor, & Mary his Wife, late M. Morton. Spr.	Augt 11.	July
90	Lock.	Frances 1st Daughter of John Lock, Taylor & Mary his Wife, late M. Ledger Spr.	Augt 13.	July 22.
91.	Balls.	Ann 1st Daughter of Samuel Balls, Coachman & Charlotte his Wife, late C. Speer. Spr.	Augt 18.	June 27.
92	Dogwell	Mary Ann Elizabeth, 2nd Daughter of John Dogwell, Gardener, & Sophia his Wife, late S. Kingstone. Spr.	Augt 24.	July 21.
93	Painter.	Harriott 1st Daughter of John Painter Labourer, & Martha his Wife, late M. Jenner. Spr.	Augt 27.	Augt 2
94	Langhorn.	William 1st Son of Henry Langhorn Esqr & Mary Ann his Wife, late M. A. Box. Spr.	Augt 28.	July 23.

Plate 5   Clapham Baptism Register, 1802

The African Academy set up by Zachary Macaulay at his house on Clapham Common provided an education for free Africans from Sierra Leone who were then to return to their land as missionaries. Unlike the Lambeth baptisms of black people who were almost exclusively servants and slaves, the Clapham register here for July 31 shows that the Academy included the sons of local kings and tribal rulers.

Cheap Repository.

THE
BLACK PRINCE,

A TRUE STORY;

Being an Account of the Life and Death of

NAIMBANNA,

AN AFRICAN KING's SON,

Who arrived in England ia the Year 1791, and set sail on his
return in June, 1793.

SOLD BY J. EVANS & SON,

(Printers to the CHEAP REPOSITORY for Moral and Religious
Tracts) No. 42, *Long-lane, West-smithfield;* and J.
HATCHARD, No. 190, *Piccadilly, London;* by J. BINNS,
Bath:—And by all Booksellers, Newsmen, and Hawkers io
Town and Country.

. *Great allowance will be made to Shopkeepers and Hawkers*
Price ONE PENNY, or 6s. 6d. per Hundred.

Entered at Stationers'-Hall.

Plate 6 "The Black Prince", title page, (1795)

This account of the life of Naimbana in England was published shortly after his death. The plate illustrates a story in the account where he witnessed a man ill treating a horse; he wished to get a gun to shoot the man. "As soon however as a passage of scripture, which condemned violence was mentioned to him, his anger ceased, and he became sorry for it".

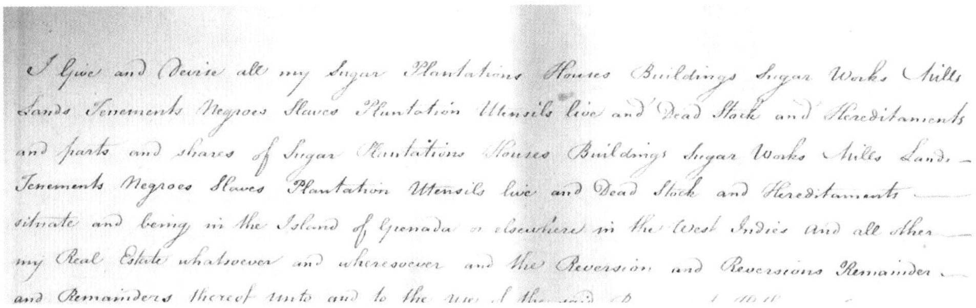

I Give and Devise all my Sugar Plantations Houses Buildings Sugar Works Mills Lands Tenements Negroes Slaves Plantation Utensils live and Dead Stock and Hereditaments and parts and shares of Sugar Plantations Houses Buildings Sugar Works Mills Lands Tenements Negroes Slaves Plantation Utensils live and Dead Stock and Hereditaments situate and being in the Island of Grenada or elsewhere in the West Indies And all other my Real Estate whatsoever and wheresoever and the Reversion and Reversions Remainder and Remainders thereof unto and to the use of the ...

Plate 7   The Will of John Hankey of Streatham, 1771

This extract from Hankey's will, leaving his slaves and negroes on his sugar plantations in Grenada in the Caribbean to his son, is a reminder of how widespread the slave economy had become by the late eighteenth century. A number of established families living in Streatham and Clapham owed their high standard of living to slave-derived wealth.

Plate 8   Price's Palm Oil Candles advertisement, ca. 1850

Price's was a local candle-maker based in Vauxhall who developed a new candle made from West African palm oil. They used the fashionable anti-slavery mood of the 1840s and 1850s as a way to promote their products. The advertisement shows the candle maker burning through the slaver's rope with his palm oil candle while offering the newly-freed slave the red cap of liberty. The message was that by purchasing Price's candles made from palm oil you were providing West Africa with an alternative trading economy to that of slavery; it was an early example of "ethical" advertising.

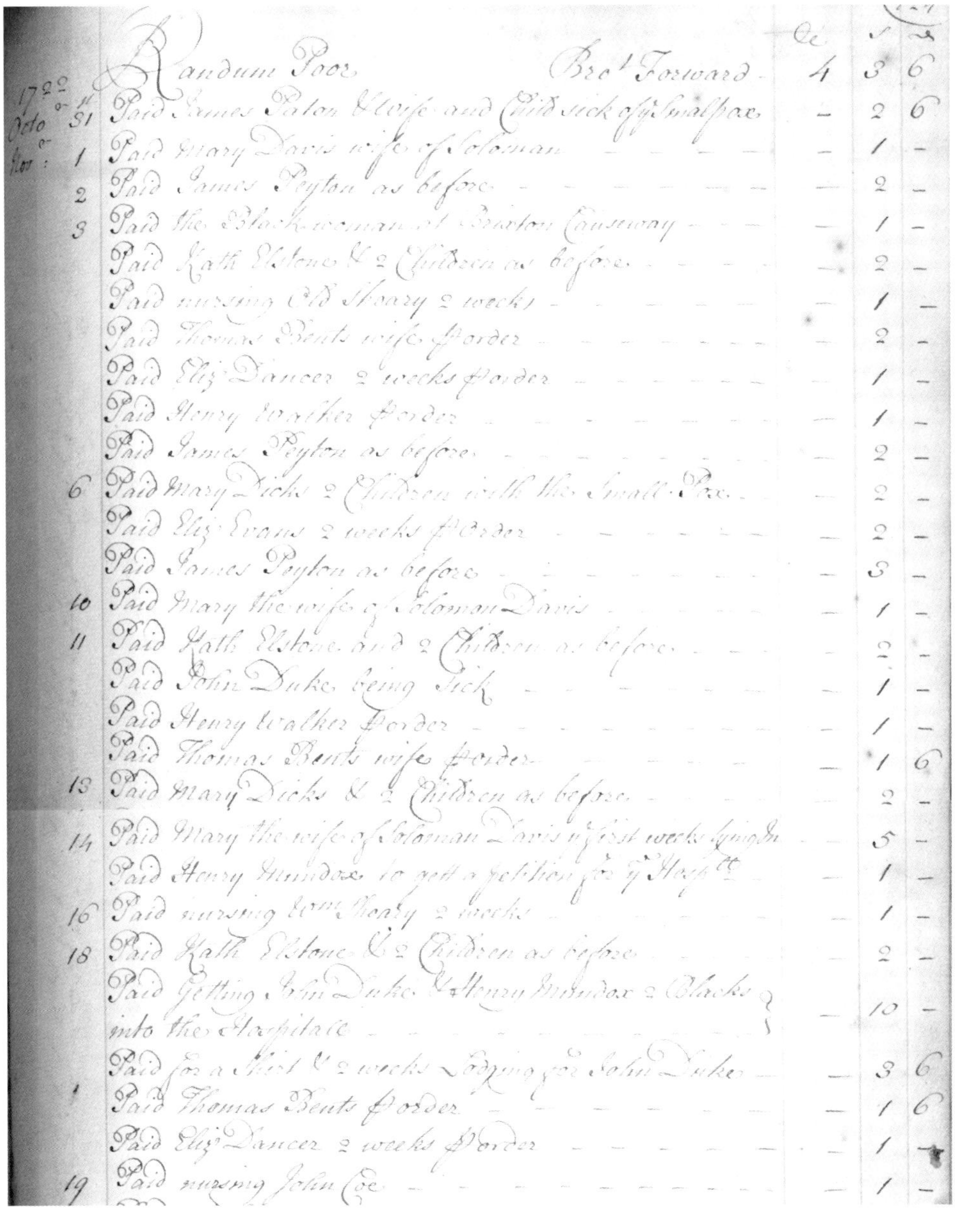

Date	Item	£	s	d
	Randum Poor — Bro.t Forward	4	3	6
1722 Octo 31	Paid James Paton & wife and Child sick of ye Smallpox	—	2	6
Nov 1	Paid Mary Davis wife of Soloman	—	1	—
2	Paid James Peyton as before	—	2	—
3	Paid the Black woman at Brixton Causeway	—	1	—
	Paid Kath Elstone & 2 Children as before	—	2	—
	Paid nursing Old Hoary 2 weeks	—	1	—
	Paid Thomas Bents wife p order	—	2	—
	Paid Eliz Dancer 2 weeks p order	—	1	—
	Paid Henry Walker p order	—	1	—
	Paid James Peyton as before	—	2	—
6	Paid Mary Dicks 2 Children with the Small Pox	—	2	—
	Paid Eliz Evans 2 weeks p Order	—	2	—
	Paid James Peyton as before	—	3	—
10	Paid Mary the wife of Soloman Davis	—	1	—
11	Paid Kath Elstone and 2 Children as before	—	2	—
	Paid John Duke being Sick	—	1	—
	Paid Henry Walker p order	—	1	—
	Paid Thomas Bents wife p order	—	1	6
13	Paid Mary Dicks & 2 Children as before		2	—
14	Paid Mary the wife of Soloman Davis ye first weeks lying In		5	—
	Paid Henry Mundox to get a petition for ye Hosp.ll	—	1	—
16	Paid nursing Tom Hoary 2 weeks	—	1	—
18	Paid Kath Elstone & 2 Children as before	—	2	—
	Paid getting John Duke & Henry Mundox 2 Blacks into the Hospitall	—	10	—
	Paid for a Shirt & 2 weeks Lodging for John Duke	—	3	6
	Paid Thomas Bents p order	—	1	6
	Paid Eliz Dancer 2 weeks p order	—	1	—
19	Paid nursing John Coe	—	1	—

Plate 9 St Mary Lambeth Church Wardens' Accounts, 1722

This page from the "Randum Poor" accounts shows three separate black people in receipt of relief in November 1722. John Duke (11 & 18 Nov), Henry Mundox (14 & 18 Nov) and "the Black woman of Brixton Causeway" (3 Nov) all receive payments for being sick or, in the woman's case, for helping nurse her baby.

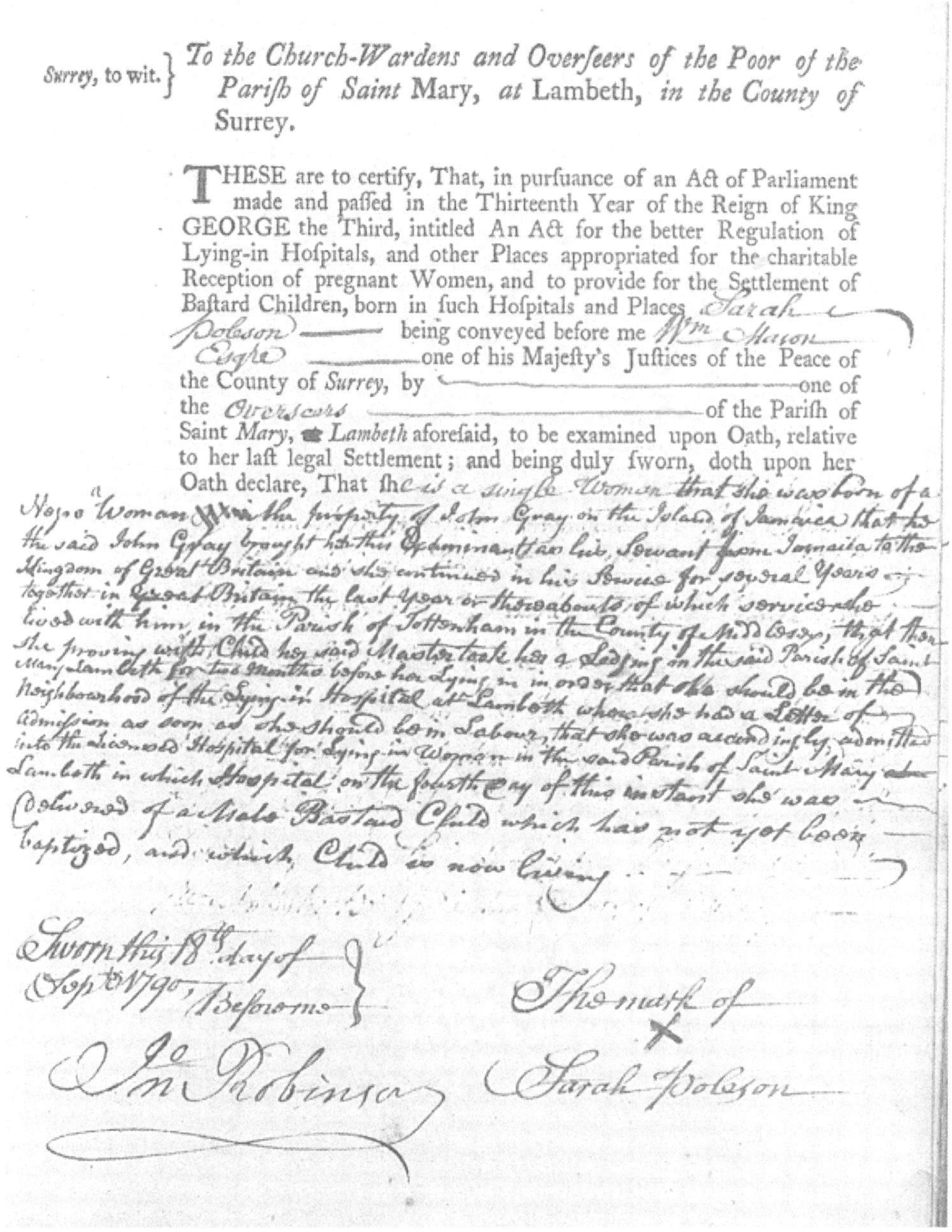

To the Church-Wardens and Overseers of the Poor of the Parish of Saint Mary, at Lambeth, in the County of Surrey.

THESE are to certify, That, in pursuance of an Act of Parliament made and passed in the Thirteenth Year of the Reign of King GEORGE the Third, intitled An Act for the better Regulation of Lying-in Hospitals, and other Places appropriated for the charitable Reception of pregnant Women, and to provide for the Settlement of Bastard Children, born in such Hospitals and Places *Sarah Poleson* ———— being conveyed before me *Wm Mason Esqre* ————— one of his Majesty's Justices of the Peace of the County of *Surrey*, by ————————————— one of the *Overseers* ————————— of the Parish of Saint *Mary*, at *Lambeth* aforesaid, to be examined upon Oath, relative to her last legal Settlement; and being duly sworn, doth upon her Oath declare, That *she is a single Woman that she was born of a Negro Woman who was the property of John Gray on the Island of Jamaica that the said John Gray brought her this Examinant as his Servant from Jamaica to the Kingdom of Great Britain and she continued in his Service for several Years together in Great Britain the last year or thereabouts of which service she lived with him in the Parish of Tottenham in the County of Middlesex; that then she proving with Child her said Master took her a Lodging in the said Parish of Saint Mary Lambeth for two months before her lying in in order that she should be in the Neighbourhood of the Lying-in Hospital at Lambeth where she had a Letter of admission as soon as she should be in Labour, that she was accordingly admitted into the Licensed Hospital for Lying-in Women in the said Parish of Saint Mary at Lambeth in which Hospital on the fourth day of this instant she was delivered of a Male Bastard Child which has not yet been baptized, and which Child is now living.*

Sworn this 18th day of Septr 1790, Before me

Jn Robinson

The mark of ✕ Sarah Poleson

Plate 10 Settlement Examination at the Lambeth Lying-In Hospital, 1790

Sarah Poleson was a black servant, formerly from Jamaica, living with her master in Tottenham. She had come to the Lying-in hospital in Lambeth to give birth to her illegitimate child. Although very rare, settlement examinations for black people like this one do give a great deal of biographical information.

NEW
Surrey Theatre.

Acting-Manager, Mr. C. DIBDIN. Stage-Manager, Mr. GALLOTT.

Mr. GALLOTT having recovered from the severe Sprain which he met with when rehearsing in the New Melo-Drame, (announced last Week, but not-performed on that account) will have honor to resume his Professional Duties.

The Part of Jocko by Mr. Ridgway.---Mons. Gouffe's Exhibition.

Composer and Leader of the Band, Mr. ERSKINE. Ballet Master, Mr. RIDGWAY.

MONDAY, JULY 11th, 1825, AND FOLLOWING EVENINGS,

(First Time,) a New Melo-Drame, in Three Acts, (written by Mr. C. DIBDIN,) with entirely New Music & Scenery, New Dresses & Decorations, Called,

BLACK CÆSAR;
Or, THE FATAL THICKET.

The Overture and Music composed by Mr. Erskine.——The Pantomimic Action directed by Mr. Ridgway.

Black Cæsar, Mr. RIDGWAY. Jack Jib, a Tar for all Weathers, Mr. GALLOTT. Bertrand, an Overseer of a Plantation, Mr. ARIS.
Fuddle, a Magistrate, Mr. T. B. CLIFFORD. Officer of Police, Mr. HENNING. Jailor, Mr. LLOYD. Nero, a Slave, Mr. SMITH.
Bardius, a Peasant, Mr. TURNER. Tumaso, a Slave, Mr. GRIFFIN. Peasants, &c. Messrs. BOULANGER, GOUGH, &c. with Supernumeraries.
Phœbe, a persecuted Slave, Miss LOUIS. Peasants and Slaves, Mrs. ARIS, Misses A. FAIRBROTHER, LANCASTER, MANNING, MERRITT, &c.

AT THE CONCLUSION OF THE FIRST ACT A BALLET,
Composed by Mr. RIDGWAY.

Performed by Mess. G. & T. Ridgway, Boulanger, Turner, Gough, Griffin. Misses Fairbrother, Rountree, A. Fairbrother, Lancaster, Manning, Merritt.

The SCENERY Designed and Painted by Mr. Tomkins, will Exhibit,

ACT I.—Scene 1.—Brilliant Panoramic View of a Plantation, 2. Interior of Bertrand's Cottage, 3. The Fatal Thicket.
4. Romantic Landscape, 5. The Plantation.
ACT II.—Scene 1.—A Justice Room. 2. Interior of the Fatal Thicket. 3. Landscape and Lake. 4. The Justice Room.
5. Entrance to the Felon's Prison. 6. Interior of the Prison.
ACT III.—Scene1—Interior of the Thicket. 2.WoodyGlen. 3. RichLandscape. 4. TheGlen. 5. TerrificCluster of Rocks & Waterfall.
The Piece concludes with an AWFUL FEATURE of RETRIBUTIVE VENGEANCE.

SINGING by Messrs. PAYNE, SMITH, and BRYANT.

To which will be added, a Burletta, altered from a Popular Piece, Entitled, The

HYPOCHONDRIAC

Megrim, Mr. MORTIMER. Denison, Mr. T. B. CLIFFORD. James, Mr. VALE. Bailiff, Mr. LLOYD. Annette, Mrs. YOUNG.

In the Piece, "WHEN A LITTLE FARM WE KEEP," by Mr. Vale & Mrs. Young.

A GRAND PAS DE QUATRE,
(Composed by Mr. RIDGWAY,) By the Three Masters RIDGWAY, and Master CICHINI.

The Entertainments to conclude with (32d Time) the Popular Melo-Drame, Called,

JOCKO
Or, THE OURANG-OUTANG OF BRAZIL.
The Music by Mr. ERSKINE.

Principal Characters.—The Jocko, (first time) Mr. RIDGWAY. Fernandez, Farmer of the Portuguese Revenues at Brazil, Mr. CLIFFORD.
Fernand, his Infant Son, Miss YOUNG. Pedro, Overseer of the Rice Plantations of Fernandez, Mr. T. B. CLIFFORD.
Dominique, his Son, Mr. VALE. Principal Slave, Mr. LLOYD. Sailors, Messrs. TURNER and GRIFFIN.
Cora, a Creole Slave of Fernandez, Mrs. SEARLE.

In Act I, a NEW BALLET, (composed by Mrs. SEARLE, the Music by Mr. SIMON,) in which will be Performed
AN INDIAN PAS DE TROIS, by Mrs. SEARLE, Misses FAIRBROTHER and RAINE.
Other Principal Dancers,
Misses RICKY, BILLING, FOSTER, and PHILLIPS, (Pupils of Mrs. SEARLE,) Misses ROUNTREE, A. FAIRBROTHER, LANCASTER, MANNING and MERRITT.

Monsieur GOUFFE,
Who has received such universal Applause, as a Brazilian Ape, will be introduced in the Piece, and Perform
His Extraordinary Jumps and Feats of Posturing, and conclude his Exhibition by
Running Round the Auditory, upon the Half-Inch Beading of the Boxes & Gallery.

The Choruses got up by Mrs. Aris. The Dresses, by Mr. Lyon & Miss Freelove. The Decorations, by Mr. Maxwell. The Machinery, by Mr. Keys.

Boxes 4s. Pit 2s. Gal. 1s. Doors open at Half-past 5, and begin at Half-past Six. Second Price at Half-past 8.
Places and Private Boxes (which have been splendidly decorated and newly furnished) may be engaged by the Night or Season, on Application to
Mr. PARKER, Box Book-keeper, at the Box Office, from 11 till 4; or of Mr. SAMS, Royal Library, St. James's Street.
Free Admissions for the Season, transferable, or not transferable, may be purchased by Application to Mr. G. Lewis, Treasurer, at the Treasury of the Theatre.
The Public are most respectfully informed, that Mr. MATSON's Coach calls Every Evening at HONEYMAN'S Coffee House, to convey
Passengers to Deptford and Greenwich. [T. Romney, Printer, Lambeth.]

Plate 11 Surrey Theatre Playbill, June 1825
This double bill at the Surrey in Blackfriars Road, shows just how popular slave melodramas were in the early nineteenth century. "Black Caesar" is set on a Caribbean plantation and "Jocko" on a Portuguese slave plantation in Brazil.

ROYAL GARDENS, VAUXHALL.

UNDER the PATRONAGE of HER MAJESTY,
H.R.H. PRINCE ALBERT, and the ROYAL FAMILY.

Director, .. Mr. ROBERT WARDELL.

WHIT-MONDAY, JUNE 12th, 1848,
And Every Evening, except Saturday.

The Lessee has the honor to announce to the Nobility and Gentry, Patrons of Vauxhall, that he has, at an immense outlay, secured the eminent services of a party of

SIX HIGHLY-TALENTED

ETHIOPIAN SERENADERS

UNDER THE DIRECTION OF

Mr. G. W. PELL

The celebrated BONE PLAYER, (late of the St. James's Theatre) including a genuine Son of the Southern clime.

JUBA

The inimitable JUBA!

He is a perfect Phenomenon, who (among other Terpsichorean Feats) accomplishes with the most perfect ease the extraordinary number of

200 DIFFERENT STEPS!

And here it may be stated, that he is the ONLY YOUTH of COLOUR that has ever visited this Country for the purpose of delineating **NEGRO LIFE AND CHARACTER.**

HE IS THUS DESCRIBED by "BOZ"

"Suddenly the lively Hero dashes in to the rescue. Instantly the fiddler grins, and goes at it tooth and nail; there is new energy in the tambourine; new laughter in the dancers; new brightliness in the very candles. Single shuffle, double shuffle, cut and cross-cut; snapping his fingers, rolling his eyes, turning in his knees, presenting the backs of his legs in front, spinning about on his toes and heels like nothing but the man's fingers on the tambourine; dancing with two left legs, two right legs, two wooden legs, two wire legs, two spring legs—all sorts of legs and no legs—what is this to him? And in what walk of life, or dance of life, does man ever get such stimulating applause as thunders about him, when, having danced his partner off her feet, and himself too, he finishes by calling for something to drink, with the chuckle of a million of counterfeit Jim Crows, in one inimitable sound."—Dickens's American Notes.

The other Serenaders include

Mr T. F. BRIGGS, Mr J. H. EVERTON
Mr J. W. VALENTINE
AND
Mr M. C. LUDLOW.

Plate 12 "The Inimitable Juba"; Vauxhall Gardens playbill, June 1848

The American dancer William Henry Lane was one of the first black entertainers to appear in Lambeth. He performed the summer season at Vauxhall Gardens in 1848 and at the Surrey Theatre the following year.

JUBA AT VAUXHALL.

The only national dance that we really believe in, as a fact, is that of the
Niggers. We mistrust the " Cachucha "—that is to say, whenever we have seen
it performed by a real Spanish *danseuse*, we have always pronounced it far inferior to Duvernay's in the " Diable Boiteux." We should never expect to see
the " Redowa " danced in its own country as Cerito and St. Leon represent
it at Her Majesty's Theatre; and we have some doubt as to whether Carlotta
Grisi's delicious " Truandaise " was ever known in the Cour des Miracles of old
Paris. Hornpipes are entirely confined to nautical dramas and pantomimes, or
the square bit of board or patch of carpet of the street dancer; and anything so
physically painful, not to say almost impossible, as those peculiar *pas* of the
Chinese that we chance to have witnessed in Europe convince us that at all
events the execution must be exceedingly limited.

Plate 13 "Juba At Vauxhall Gardens", Illustrated London News, 1848

Master Juba was one of the first black performers to be appreciated for his talent rather than just because he was black. Initially
reviewed by Charles Dickens in New York, he attracted rave reviews in London.

Plate 14 "Lancelott's Ethiopian Quadrille", Vauxhall Gardens music sheet, ca. 1840

"Black" musical acts were very fashionable by the 1840s. But apart from the caricature depiction of black people on the cover,
it is unlikely that there was anything Ethiopian about this re-packaging of traditional dance music.

Plate 15 Black Musicians at Vauxhall Gardens, ca 1840
The black musicians performing in England from the 1840s were Afro-American in the main, typically playing banjo, tambourine and bones.

Plate 16 "Nine O'clock p.m.: House of Call for the Victoria Audience" 1859
The Victoria Theatre in Waterloo Road, latterly the Old Vic, was one of the main Lambeth theatres. Its audience here includes a black sailor; and the crowd is being entertained by a black banjo player in top hat and wing collar.

HONOR TO LORD NAPIER

ASTLEY'S

THEATRE ROYAL.

Licensed by the Lord Chamberlain to Mr. W. H. C. Nation, 20, King Street, St James's.

ON SATURDAY, SEPTEMBER 12th, 1868,

Will be performed, for the first time, an entirely original, historical, Grand Naval and Military Spectacular Drama, in Four Parts, replete with Military Evolutions, Processions, Dances, Pageants, Combats, &c., entitled the

THE CONQUEST
OF
MAGDALA

FALL OF THEODORE !

The whole of the Picturesque Scenery (from Drawings taken on the spot) by

MR. JULIAN HICKS, MR. J. W. HALL, AND ASSISTANTS.

Founded on the recent Glorious Expedition into Abyssinia, undertaken by the British Government and sanctioned by the British People, with the humane and noble purpose of rescuing numerous Captives from the hands of a ferocious Tyrant, this Drama Essays to depict some of the most striking scenes, brilliant incidents, and deeds of arms in the memorable Campaign. To heighten the dramatic interest of the Piece, and relieve by it broad humour and pathos, some characters are introduced which, though they owe their existence entirely to the author's imagination, are not incompatible with the facts of contemporary history. A more extraordinary March than that accomplished by the British Troops is not on record since the days of Alexander the Great; and the achievement of traversing 400 miles of rocky pass and wilderness, followed by a battle and a siege, and crowned by the Rescue of the Prisoners, and the exercise of mercy and humanity towards the Widowed Queen and Orphan Child of the execrable Despot, is without a parallel in modern times.

To provide an intelligible motive for the cruelty of Theodore, the King, beyond those which history assigns to him, a Prologue has been written, which supplies the Tyrant with the additional excuse of the prescription of his ancestors.

DRAMATIS PERSONÆ.

THE PROLOGUE.—ABYSSINIA 200 YEARS AGO.

Abdul	(a Mahometan Chieftain)	MR. G. VINCENT
Rasselas	(his Son—with Songs)	MR. FLTON
Haly, Tigro, and Hamet	(Abyssinians)	Messrs. BUTLER, BENTLEY, & ROSS
Captain Tarleton		MR. SYMONDSON
Jedediah Snuffleton	(a Puritan)	MR. J. DANNAVILLE
Timothy Flowertop	(a Sutler) ... MR. J. ROYSTON	Margery ... (his Wife) ... MRS. MACKNEY

ABYSSINIANS, SOLDIERS OF LORD PETERBOROUGH, &c.

THE DRAMA.

ABYSSINIA AT THE PRESENT DAY.

Theodore	(King of Abyssinia)	MR. BRANDON ELLIS
Theodora	(his Queen)	MISS M. SAUNDERS
Manilek	(a Renegade Chief)	MR. WALTER CARLE
Ahmed	(a Chief)	MR. DANNAVILLE
Kassa ... (a young Chief) ... MISS MACKNEY	Alameio... (the Son of Theodore)	MISS ANNIE
A Gorilla ...	MR. TOM LAMB (the celebrated representative of the Monkey Tribe)	
The Chief of Bedouins		MR. BUTLER

Abyssinian Warriors, Banner Bearers, Dancing Girls, Mule Drivers, Priests, &c., by a numerous Corps of Auxiliaries.

THE BRITISH.

Lieutenant-General Sir Robert Napier, K.C.B.	(the Commander-in-Chief of the Expedition)	MR. H. J. BROUGHTON
Lieutenant Lightfoot	(of the Royal Naval Brigade)	MISS MARION
Captain Harcourt	(a British Captive)	MR. J. GARDINER
Alexander Vattel	(a Cook and Barber to the King)	MR. J. ROYSTON
Paddy Shannon	(a Corporal in the Royal Artillery)	MR. G. VINCENT
Timothy Scroggins	(a Private in the 4th Foot)	MR. GEORGE YARNOLD
Tom Breezy	(a Boatswain in the Royal Navy)	MR. R. YOUNG
An Old Man and other Captives ...	MESSRS. SYMONDSON, WILTON, WALKER, &c.	
Tabitha Bramberry	(Maid of Honour to the Queen)	MISS EMILY SCOTT
Sergeant Snapton	MR. ROSS Officer	MR. WILLIAMS

Plate 17 "The Conquest of Magdala", 1868

Re-enactments of recent military events made for popular theatre in Lambeth. Here the invasion of Ethiopia, by the British Army under Sir Robert Napier and the defeat and suicide of the Emperor Theodore is "celebrated" at Astleys' Amphitheatre five months after the event.

The British Soldiers of the 4th and 33rd Regiments will be represented by a

A LARGE BODY OF THE GRENADIER GUARDS

Especially engaged. The Scinde Horse and Beloochee Cavalry will be personified by numerous Trained Equestrians Mounted on

A SUPERB STUD OF HORSES.

PROGRAMME OF THE SCENERY.

PROLOGUE 1660.

A MOUNTAIN DEFILE & VALLEY IN ABYSSINIA

TWO HUNDRED YEARS AGO.

Conflict between Abyssinians and the Soldiers of Lord Peterborough.

Mr. ELTON will Sing and a New Martial Song written by Mr. SIDDONS and set to Music by Mr. CORRI.

THE DRAMA 1868.

ACT I.—GARDENS AND KIOSK IN THE ROYAL PALACE.

Grand PROCESSION of Mounted WARRIOR CHIEFS, Banner Bearers.

An ABYSSINIAN DANCE by the Corps de Ballet, arranged by Mr. ALEXANDRE JAY.

ACT II. ANNESLEY BAY & ZOOLLA

SPLENDIDLY ILLUSTRATING THE

ARRIVAL AND LANDING OF THE BRITISH TROOPS AND SEAMEN.

MILITARY MOVEMENTS AND EVOLUTIONS.

HORNPIPE BY THE WHOLE OF THE NAVAL BRIGADE.

A FOREST. SCIENTIFIC RESEARCHES.

NATURAL HISTORY—THE GORILLA—MAN *VERSUS* MONKEY.

RUINS OF THE ROCK-CUT TEMPLE OF DONGOLO.

The Rites of the Wandering Tribe—Peril of the Queen & Prince—their Rescue by the British—Hazardous condition of the too curious Scroggins.

ACT III.—THE PASS AT AROGIE.

BATTLE between the ADVANCED GUARD of the BRITISH

AND THE ABYSSINIANS.

THE TENT OF SIR ROBERT NAPIER.

THE LIBERATED CAPTIVES—THE PROTECTED QUEEN.

HALL IN THE KING'S PALACE.

Before the Fortress of Magdala

THE BATTLE! THE STORM!! THE CAPTURE!!!

DEATH OF THEODORE.

DISTINGUISHED GALLANTRY OF THE 33rd REGIMENT!

Sir ROBERT NAPIER Protects the Child of Theodore

The New and Original Music (written for the occasion) by

MR. WILLIAM CORRI.

The superb and accurate Costumes by Mr. S. MAY, Miss YATES, and Mr. CANDLAN. The Mechanical Effects by Mr. ROBERT GILBERT and Assistants.

Preceded by Mr. SUTER'S Farce of

PECULIAR PEOPLE-VERY

Musical Director - Mr. W. CORRI. Acting Manager - Mr. COOPER.
PRICES—Gallery, 6d. Pit, 1s. Upper Boxes, 1s. 6d. Lower Boxes, 2s. Balcony, 3s.
Orchestra Stall Chairs, 5s. Private Boxes, £1 1s. and upwards. Box office open daily,
under the direction of Mr. DRYSDALE, from 11 till 4. Private Boxes, Stalls, and Places may also be
secured at Messrs. Mitchell's, Bubb's, etc., Bond Street. Doors open at Half-past Six, commence at Seven o'clock,
precisely.

WILKES & POLLARD, Steam Printers, 63, Newington Butts, S.E.

Plate 18 "The Conquest of Magdala", 1868
Continuation of the Astley's Amphitheatre playbill.

BOWER SALOON

Stangate Street, Westminster Road, Six Doors from the Canterbury Hall.

Licensed by the Lord Chamberlain to VICTOR HAZLETON, Bower Saloon, Upper Marsh, Lambeth. Manager, ... Mr W. D. HARLEY.

BOXES - 6d. PIT - 4d. GALLERY - 2d. Half-price at Nine o'clock.

BOXES - 3d. PIT - 2d.

☞ NEW & IMPORTANT ENGAGEMENTS ☜

The Management have, at a considerable expense, arranged for a limited number of Nights, with the Celebrated and Original

SAVANNAH MINSTRELS!

The Troupe consists of SEVEN first-class Singers, Musicians, and Comedians, who are pronounced by the entire London Press to be the BEST, most refined, and mirth-creating entertainers who have appeared in the Metropolis. The Entertainment is of a refined yet racy character, and entirely different to any which has preceded it ; comprising

Songs, Duets, Glees, Refined Negro Dances, Music, Vocal and Instrumental.

THE SAVANNAH TROUPE CONSISTS OF THE FOLLOWING ARTISTES

Mr. WALLACE   Mr HANKEYSON   Mr. TALBOT
Mr. EDMONDS   Mr. KING   Mr. HOLLINGSWORTH

WASHINGTON SELBY, THE AMERICAN PRIZE JIG DANCER.

Acknowledged to be the Greatest Wonder of the World.

Solo Violinist - - - - - - - - - Mr. TALBOT.

Miss MARY FIELDING

THE POPULAR AND VERSATILE ACTRESS, FOR A LIMITED NUMBER OF NIGHTS.

MISS CLARA GRIFFITHS.

THE CHARMING SOUBRETTE, IN A NEW CHARACTER; AND

MR. GEORGE PEARCE, EVERY EVENING.

ON MONDAY SEPT. 16th, 1861, and every Evening during the Week,

THE PERFORMANCES WILL COMMENCE WITH A POWERFUL DRAMA, REPLETE WITH INTEREST, entitled

EDGAR OF RAVENSWOOD

OR A MERMAID'S WELL, & THE FATAL PROPHECY.

Sir William Ashton ... Mr HENRI   Colonel Ashton ... Mr CLIFTON   Henry Ashton ... Miss HEMMINGS
Edgar, Master of Ravenswood - - - Mr GEORGE PEARCE,
Hayston of Buckland ..... Mr H. VINCENT   Captain Craigengelt .... Mr T. BYRNE   Lockard .... Mr OLEWY
Lady Ashton ..... Miss LOUISA GLANVILLE
Lucy Ashton - - - - Miss MARY FIELDING

TO BE FOLLOWED BY THE

SAVANNAH MINSTRELS'

ENTERTAINMENT.

SELECTIONS FROM

The Creole Girl | Minnie Bell | Let us all united be
The Corn Fields | Angelina Baker | Whose dat Foot a
Rosa Bell | Long Ago | burning
Hen Convention | Where are my School- | What's dat Noise in
Whilst I was Walking | mates gone | de Kitchen
Darling Bessie | Ella Leene | Composed expressly for the Savannah
Come another Day | Oh! Boys, Sing the Song | Minstrels, by H Bonner, Esq.

The Entertainment will conclude with the Celebrated

OLD BILLY PATTERSON!

Composed expressly for this Company, by J. H. TULLY, Esq.

THE WHOLE TO CONCLUDE WITH THE

PEASANT AND THE HEIRESS

OR WOMAN'S LOVE.

Francois - - - Miss MARY FIELDING

Plate 19 Savannah Minstrels, Bower Saloon playbill, September 1863

By the 1860s "nigger minstrel" performances were extremely popular. The music and performance style derived from the Southern US states and had become particularly topical to English audiences because of the Civil War in America. However, many of the acts in London, including, probably, the Savannah Minstrels here, were actually Europeans made up as "black-face" acts.

4 Local Newspapers

There were no local newspapers printed in Lambeth in the eighteenth century. The concept of a local suburban press is a mid-nineteenth century one. Before that date newspapers were an expensive, highly taxed commodity for a literate minority. In Lambeth people would have read London newspapers that reported a mixture of national, international and local London news.

In the eighteenth century London was still the largest of England's three slave ports in front of Bristol and Liverpool. The slave trade and the slave economy was an ever-present fact of life and source of news stories and advertising. The London press frequently contained notices for auctions and sales of individual slaves. Later on these would start to be outnumbered by announcements of rewards for runaway and escaped slaves.

In a typical example, *The Public Advertiser* of 1762, includes an advertisement for the entertainments at Vauxhall Gardens alongside one notice for the auction sale
of sugar, coffee and cocoa, being the cargo of St. Anthony from Guadeloupe
and another for the sale
by the candle… of the good ship Cato with twenty nine-pounder guns, a very fast sailer, square stern, plantation built, burden 300 tons more or less with excellent dimensions for the Guinea or West India Trade, has a very large inventory and is a fine ship for the transport service.
The word slavery is not mentioned in either notice but the implications are clear. Sugar, coffee and cocoa from the Caribbean were all slave-worked, plantation crops at this date. In the notice of the sale of the *Cato*, the "transport service" and "the Guinea and West Indian Trade" (whose only trade at that date was in human beings) are the clues that the ship for sale is a slaver.[77]

It was not until the 1840's that a local Lambeth press starts to emerge. Dozens of short-run titles appeared throughout the nineteenth century representing all shades of political opinion and local interest. The sole survivor today, *The South London Press,* was first published in 1865; but there were more than 20 other local titles, many serving very specific smaller areas like Brixton or Clapham that have now ceased.

---

[77] *The Public Advertiser,* July 12 1762

It was never going to be possible to search the entire local press for the nineteenth century and the research was concentrated on the earliest short-run papers and samples from some of the others. A considerable amount more work could be done in this area.

Taking a very broad interpretation of what constituted "black and Asian" news stories, the results obtained were interesting and extremely diverse. They included a large amount of reporting on national and international news as well as the more familiar items about local events, entertainment and crime that we associate with the press today. The regular, detailed news reports and editorial coverage of events like the Indian Mutiny and the survival of the West African slave trade was one of the more surprising elements found in the early local press. The Jamaica rebellion of 1865 and the suppression and massacres carried out by the British after the event received heated coverage in South London as did various local meetings convened to protest about the events.[78]

The Abolitionist movement in the USA in the 1850s and 1860s was very effective in getting its message out and there are regular reprinted stories in South London papers taken from the liberal US press about their campaigns. These include reports of meetings of The Negro Emancipation Society in London as well as some very emotive accounts of the ill treatment of slaves in the South, demonstrating that the slavery debate remained an important issue long after abolition in Britain .[79] One of the most curious post-abolition accounts is the visit to England in 1892 of an elderly former slave, Martha Ann Rix, who travelled five hundred miles from Liberia to be introduced to Queen Victoria at Windsor and have lunch with the Lord Mayor of London. The reports of the visit and the publication of her grateful letters of thanks upon her return home seem to have been something of a sentimental public relations triumph, confirming the English image of themselves as the true friend of the slave. It was reported widely and presumably not just in *The Brixtonian*.[80]

This world view was reinforced by the reporting of an extremely large number of lectures and meetings about black issues that were taking place in Lambeth and South London. Regular topics included accounts of missionary work in Africa and Asia,

---

[78] *South London Press*, 4, 18 Nov., 2, 9, 16 Dec. 1865, *Clapham Gazette*, 1 Dec.1865, 1 Jan. 1866
[79] *South London Journal*, 8 Dec 1855, 5 Aug. & 30 Sept. 1856, 25 Aug. 1857, 16 Apr. 1859
[80] *The Brixtonian*, 16 & 23 July., 10 & 24 Sept. 1892

travel, exploration and colonial conquest by participants who had recently returned to England. Some of the speakers were themselves black. In 1864 the Reverend Samuel Crowther spoke to the Clapham branch of the Church Missionary Society about his own life and his work in West Africa.[81] In 1888 a Jamaican Methodist pastor, F E Marston, was at the Boro' Road chapel in Southwark preaching and appealing for money to open more churches in Jamaica.[82]

Equally numerous in the 1850s and 1860s were press reports of local talks and readings about slavery. These included many local appearances by former slaves: Mary E. Webb, "a lady of colour, from the United States", gave a public reading from *Uncle Tom's Cabin* in Greenwich; Henry Box Brown, an escaped slave appeared at venues in South London describing his experiences as did the Reverend Sella Martin, also from the USA . A lot of the impetus for this was religious and there are frequent reports of speakers at local mission societies and bible societies discussing the links between evangelical Christianity and the anti slavery movement.[83] The topic was still newsworthy at the end of the century when a Mr J Dickerson appeared at Brixton Hall giving the narrative of "My life as a Slave"; he also sang John Brown's "Emancipation Song" to the audience.[84]

There clearly were some London and local black celebrities. Mary Seacole's benefit concerts at the Royal Surrey Gardens in 1857 and Ira Aldridge's return to the London stage in 1865 were enthusiastically reported as were the various visits of royalty like the Prince of Scinde, the Queen of Oude and the Queen of the Sandwich Islands (who actually visited Clapham). Entertainment was another defined area that black people were deemed to occupy, and the press coverage of this has been described in the previous chapter. However there appears to have been very little between, at one extreme, news stories about black celebrities, entertainers and churchmen and, at the other, black people as the perpetrators or victims of crime.

Not all the local press chose to report crime. Some of the more serious journals confined themselves to report and comment on national and international news and reporting on the activities of the various arms of local government. Before 1865 there are very few local crime stories. But in that year *The South London Press* started with

[81] *Clapham Gazette,* 1 May 1864
[82] *Westminster & Lambeth Gazette*, 25 Aug. 1888
[83] *South London Journal*, 23 Dec. 1856, 6 Jan. and 7 Apr. 1857; *South London Press*, 4 Nov. 1865

what we might recognise today as a much more familiar, "tabloid" approach to local news with reports about murders, robberies, suicides, assaults and accidental deaths. In the three and a half years of *The South London Press* sampled from February 1865 to August 1868 there were twelve local reports of crimes or deaths involving black people. While all twelve are described as men or women "of colour", eight of them are further described by their jobs. There were two sailors, a "preacher on slavery", a "lecturer on slavery", a "nigger musician", a "negro melodist" , an "attendant at a wild beast show" and a pauper in the casual ward of the workhouse.

While no great statistical sample, it is nevertheless interesting in apparently confirming the anecdotal evidence of many contemporary and earlier London writers by suggesting that many black people in Lambeth, or at least those who had occasion to be reported on by the local press, were still only engaged on the edges of the London economy as sailors, musicians and beggars or else still depending on their historical position as former slaves for a livelihood.

---

[84] *The Brixtonian*, 9 Feb. 1900

Lambeth Newspaper Reports, 1840 - 1900

Art of Writing	Lengthy article on Mr Mariner's account of the Tonga Islands	The Lambeth Argus	21 Mar 1840
Adventure with a Cobra de Capella	From a letter dated Kirkee, near Poonah: detailed account of encounter with Cobra	The Lambeth Argus	28 Mar 1840
Clapham Athenaeum: Notice of Lectures	Review of lecture by Dr J. Bowring on the customs and habits of the Chinese; despite the antiquity of the Chinese Empire modern Chinese have failed to keep pace with improvements of other less ancient nations	Clapham Gazette	1 Dec 1853
Gleanings: book review	Review of *Ride Through the Nubian Desert* by Captain W. Peel, which describes an encounter with an Arab. The latter reluctantly accepts an offer of vinegar thinking that it is alcohol.	Clapham Gazette	1 Dec 1853
The New Year: an essay	Compares modern Turkey with its barbarous past. The implication being that having adopted many of the ways of the 'civilised' Christian countries it is now worthy of praise.	Clapham Gazette	1 Jan 1854
Clapham Literary and Scientific Institution:	Review of lecture: "A Week in Constantinople", by Percy B. St. John; describes the customs and habits of the inhabitants of Constantinople and the 'many objectionable features' to be found there: absence of justice; the prevalence of corruption; nepotism and the evils of polygamy	Clapham Gazette	1 Feb 1854
Clapham Worthies	Biog. of William Wilberforce, advocate for the abolition of slavery and member of the Clapham Sect	Clapham Gazette	1 Apr 1854
Clapham Worthies	Biog. of Granville Sharp, advocate for the abolition of slavery and member of the Clapham Sect	Clapham Gazette	1 May 1854
How Debtors are Treated in Abyssinia	A short article describing the arbitrary way with which debtors in Abyssinia are dealt in the absence of a recognizable criminal justice system.	Clapham Gazette	1 Jun 1854
'Chinese Evangelizatio n Society'	Charles Bird, secretary of the society, describes progress on the printing of a Bible for Chinese consumption. Ends by soliciting financial support from the 'Christian Public'.	Clapham Gazette	1 Oct 1854
Slavery in the United States	Near Franklin, Tennessee, an Ellen Burden "having had her jealousy aroused by some unexplained conduct of her husband" tortured one of her slaves to an extreme display of cruelty.	South London Gazette	8 Dec 1855

Daring Highway Robbery with violence	Thomas Lebland, a young man of color, was charged with robbing and ill-using in open day, Mr. Thomas Towell, a gentleman residing in Brunswick-terrace Camberwell-road, was placed at the bar before the Hon. G.C. Norton, on Thursday, for final examination. It appeared that on Monday the 10th instant Mr. Towel was on his way home, about four o'clock in the afternoon, when the prisoner and three others were seen to follow him. In the Walworth Road the prisoner solicited charity and received a three penny piece from the prosecutor. The parties still followed him, and just as he approached his own gate and was about to open it, one of them struck him a violent blow on the back part of his head, and he instantly fell to the ground. Two of the parties then rifled his pockets, and amongst other things carried away a gold watch, chain and seals, of the value of 30 guineas. The prosecutor remained insensible for some hours from the effect of the blow, and was confined to his house for several days afterwards. The prisoner was subsequently taken into custody, when he had on several new articles of wearing apparel all of which he bought on the morning after the robbery. The prisoner was identified as one of the parties who committed the robbery, by four credible witnesses. A previous conviction was proved against the prisoner. Committed for trial. A second charge was established against the prisoner of stealing a piece of bacon, weighing 8 lbs, from the shop of Mrs. Read, cheesemonger, for which he was also committed.	South London Local Journal	25 Dec 1855
News in Brief	We have later news from the Bahamas. Salt making had commenced at Crocked Islands with every prospect of success. From Hayti we have additional particulars concerning the defeat of Soulouque by the Dominicans. The latter were armed with Minie rifles, which accounts for the great slaughter among the Haitians. Soulouque had turned up, and was concentrating his forces for another expedition. The Dominicans, however, were fully prepared to repel their enemy. All the posts were under strict blockade.	South London Gazette	23 Feb 1856
Foreign Miscellany	Accounts from Gonavas, Hayti, state that Soulesque had disabandoned his army, and that an invasion of Dominica was abandoned.	South London Gazette	15 March 1856
Arrival of Bishop Weeks at Sierra Leone	The St. Thomas incumbent becomes bishop for Sierra Leone. See also 22. Dec 1855, Vol 1 No.8, p.3	South London Gazette	22 Mar 1856
Siamese Courtship	An Englishman's interpretation of the marriage customs of Siam.	Clapham Gazette	1 Jul 1856

Political. Arrival of a Sikh Chief.	The prince of Scinde, landed at Southampton, on Saturday; he is accompanied by his *padre* , secretary, and two male servants. The object of his visit is to assist in recovering certain properties belonging to his father's territories which were taken from him by the commander of Upper Scinde, contrary as is alleged, to promises made by the late Sir Charles Napier, Commander-in-Chief of India	South London Local Journal	15 July 1856
Mary Seacole	Mrs Seacole, the celebrated proprietress of the provision store in the Crimea, intends setting up a similar establishment at Aldershot. Her fame in this particular department of business is so well known among all military men	South London Local Journal	15 July 1856
Slave Trade in the United States	We are so informed by the deputy United States' marshal, that they are well satisfied that at least 15 slave vessels have sailed from this part within the last 12 months, and three within the last three weeks. (New York Journal of Commerce)	South London Local Journal	5 Aug 1856
Fashionable	The Queen of Oude at Southampton – The Indus arrived on Wednesday evening at Southampton, with the Queen Dowager of Oude, the brother and son of the ex-King, and 106 followers. The Queen Dowager is a good-looking woman of dark complexion, fifty-five years of age, and very intelligent. She is very sanguine as to the success of her mission in this country for the restoration of her son to the Throne of Oude. She has £80, 000 for current expenses. ……..The brother of the ex-king is a fine tall man, and is a general in the Oude army. The son of the ex-King is a very handsome youth. They dress in the most magnificent style, their head-dress being covered with diamonds and emeralds. Many of their followers are small, poor-looking men, and exceedingly dark. They are shoe-makers, tailors, cooks, and of other trades. They were working all day long on board. The dishes were usually served up of curries and pilaus, […] .[85]	South London Local Journal	26 Aug 1856
Miscellaneous .	Queen Dowager of Oude and her following are in London (residing in Marylebone) since Saturday.	South London Local Journal	9 Sep 1856
The slave trade at New York	The fitting out of slavers at this port still continues. A vessel, says the New York Journal of Commerce, sailed last Saturday.	South London Local Journal	30 Sep 1856
Slavery in the United States.	2 cols. long article on the present situation in the South, Kansas, etc.	South London Local Journal	30 Sep 1856
Royal Surrey Theatre	Brilliant success of the New Grand Drama "the Half Caste".	South London Local Journal	21 Oct 1856

[85] See South London Local Journal, 2 Sep 1856 for note on the reception of her and her following at their hotel suite in Southampton, acompanied by servants and "two gigantic Nubian eunuchs".

Woolwich. Woolwich Garrison Races	On Tuesday morning the annual celebrations were held [description of races] 'The third race was run for the "Benefit Stakes", of 5 sovs each, with £40 added.' The horses ridden included ' Captain Brarazon's br. F. Mrs Seacole. 'Mrs. Seacole made steady running throughout, and won after a good race by half a length.	South London Local Journal	28 Oct 1856
Royal Surrey Theatre.	Every evening during the week "Dred".	South London Local Journal	4 Nov 1856
Royal Surrey Theatre	Every evening during the week "Dred".	South London Local Journal	11 Nov 1856
Surrey.	'The clever drama of "The Flower Girl" was received here last evening, for the first piece; "Dred" has been placed on the bottom of the bill, with Mr. Basil Potter and M. Norman in the characters of Dred and Tom Gordon, vice Creswick and Shepherd, retired from this part.'	South London Journal	18 Nov 1856
Royal Surrey Theatre	Every evening during the week "Dred".	South London Journal	2 Dec 1856
Southwark Literary Institution	A lecture by Evan B. Jones Esq. M.R.C.S. on "The varieties of the human race", very comprehensive. The Arab the most perfect of the human family.	South London Local Journal	2 Dec 1856
Royal Surrey Theatre	Every evening during the week "Dred".	South London Journal	9 Dec 1856
The slave trade in Cuba.	An American ship with 600 African slaves landed at La Punta de Teja.	South London Journal	9 Dec 1856
West Kent Guardian. Greenwich. Dramatic Reading of "Uncle Tom's Cabin" –	Mrs. Mary E. Webb, a lady of color, from the United States, gave a reading of "Uncle Tom's Cabin" at the Lecture Hall, on Thursday evening. Mrs Webb did not, it is needless to say, read the work in the shape in which it is familiar to us, but a very much condensed and dramatised version, constructed for the purpose by Mrs. Stowe. She has an agreeable voice, a good deal of feeling, and very nice discrimination. As the reading proceeded, this later quality became more apparent; the distinctive character given to each of the dramatis personae, being well marked. Uncle Tom himself was undoubtedly her most successful effort. The audience was not so large as may have been expected; but Mrs Webb's reading was unanimously pronounced to be exceedingly interesting.	South London Journal	23 Dec 1856
Croydon	Croydon on Tuesday last. Mrs Webb gave another reading at the Lecture Hall, Crown-hill.	South London Journal	6 Jan 1857
Alleged Kidnapping of Coloured Seamen – Violent Conflict -	Before the Birkenhead Magistrates: an American ship, the James L. Bogart was lying in the Mersey 'wanting a crew'. A number of seaman, incl. " coloured persons" approached the crew and asked if it was the "Robin Hood", a ship for which they had been contracted. Once on board they were put into "bronz	South London Journal	28 Jan 1857

70

Greenwich Institution – American Slavery	Tuesday last, W. C. Connon Esq. M.A. gave a lecture on slavery. […] only two British authors Alison and Carlyle – had attempted to "whitewash" slavery, and the arguments of both these writers were minutely examined and severely animadverted upon. The British travellers who had spoken of slavery were enumerated, from Miss Martiean to Mr. William Chambers, and a glowing eulogium was passed upon Mrs Stowe, whose "Uncle Tom's Cabin" first made the subject of slavery very popular on both sides of the Atlantic, and whose recent work, "Dred", was well calculated to deepen the impression made by the former work, though, from the fickleness of the reading public, was subject to fits, little was heard about it.	S London Journal	7 Apr 1857
Borough of Southwark. District News. Panorama of American Slavery.	During the last three or four months, we have had frequent occasion to repeat the popular entertainment of Mr. Henry Box Brown on the subject of American slavery. Mr. Brown's lecture includes the exhibition of a large moving panorama, delineating a number of striking incidents. The history of this man is so marvellous, that if it were not authenticated by the testimonials of respectable and competent authorities, it would probably be classed among the extravagancies [sic] of the. renowned Mr. Arrowsmith. Mr. Brown made his escape from slavery by being packed up in a box and conveyed 350 miles by railways and steamboats in 27 hours. Upon his personal experience of slavery, Mr. Brown has founded an entertainment so popular in its character, that it is spoken of in the highest terms by those who had witnessed it, and when he recently occupied the Lecture-Hall at Deptford, for several consecutive days, the audience which assembled were more numerous than had ever been seen at the hall on any similar occasion. We see by an advertisement that Mr. Brown is now at Mr. Barrett's Grammar School, Bermondsey where we wish him very success	S London Journal	7 Apr 1857
Public Amusements. Astley's	The Easter holidays are welcomed at this favourite place of public amusement by the production for the first time of a grand European and African military spectacle by Mr. C. A. Somerset, *entitled The French in Algiers*; or *The Battle of Constantine*, which enables Mr. Cook to bring upon the stage, with brilliant effect, his magnificent stud of trained horses, as well as the entire resources of his vast establishment. [etc. description of the story]	S London Journal	21 Apr 1857
Clapham 'London Missionary Society'	The report describes the extent of the society's involvement in Africa, India, the West Indies and the Pacific islands. The chairman praises the non-denominational nature of their mission.	Clapham Gazette	1 May 1857
Rough Notes of short visit to China	The article quotes extensively from a correspondent in China who describes his experiences there making a number of observations about Chinese society.	Clapham Gazette	1 Jul 1857

A Fearful Tragedy	[...] has been enacted at Sierra Leone. Captain Pearson, of the 1st West India Regiment, on the night of the 14th May lifted the screen dividing their berths in the barracks, and shot Lieut. Watson, of the 3rd West India Regiment, through the head as he lay asleep in his bed. On the previous evening, at a public entertainment the Captain played the role of Othello, Lieut. Watson played Yago, and the part of Desdemona was performed by Mrs. Fitzmaurice, the wife of another officer, who appears to have been the unfortunate cause of the said crime.	S London Journal	21 July 1857
Seacole testimonial at the Royal Surrey Gardens	A Grand Festival, in aid of Mrs. Seacole, commenced at the Royal Surrey Gardens last night, under distinguished patronage. It is to last four days, and the musical arrangements comprise eleven military bands, supported by Mr. Julien's renowned orchestra, strengthened by several of the leading vocalists of day. The military instruments amount to 600, and the total number of performers exceeds a thousand.	S London Journal	28 July 1857
The Seacole Fund – Royal Surrey Gardens	For the benefit of Mrs. Seacole, at the Royal Surrey Gardens, to commence on Monday, July 27th, 1857, and continue for four days. 1,800 performers, including 11 military bands. under the immediate Patronage of H R H the General Commanding-in-Chief, His Grace the Duke of Wellington [lists other patrons]	S London Journal	28 July 1857
The Bengal Relief Fund	An article describing the aftermath of the Indian Mutiny exhorts the readership to make subscriptions to a fund the objective of which was to alleviate the hardships of those who have suffered.	Clapham Gazette	1 Oct 1857
Employment of Girls	The article criticises the exploitation of young female labour by the 'Sepoys' of the mantle and envelope stationers' shops	Clapham Gazette	1 Nov 1857
Circulation of News in India	The article describes the system of distributing newsletters in India.	Clapham Gazette	1 Nov 1857
Storming and capturing of Delhi	A letter from an officer in the 2nd Bengal European Fusiliers describing his experience in the storming and capturing of Delhi	Clapham Gazette	1 Dec 1857
The Wants of China	The article anticipates the commercial importance of China in relation to England and describes the situation of the markets for goods etc.	Clapham Gazette	1 Jan 1858
Lecture on India	The lecture covers the history, geography, demographics and religion of India amongst other things. USPG in Foreign Parts	Clapham Gazette	1 Jan 1858
Indian Administration	The article reports on a recent memoranda issued from India House on the government of India. It explains the relationship between land tenure and revenue collection amongst other things.	Clapham Gazette	1 Mar 1858
The Relief of Lucknow	S W Partridge in his poem *The Relief of Lucknow* eulogizes the British fighting spirit in the face of adversity.	Clapham Gazette	1 Mar 1858

India	A follow on article to that of 1 Mar 1858 in which the following features of life in India are touched upon: the economy; law reform; public works and education.	Clapham Gazette	1 Apr 1858
Poem: Slavery	anti slavery poem by M.W.J.M.	Clapham Gazette	1 Jul 1858
The North American Indian	Anglo Saxon interpretation of native American home life [quoted from *Kansas* by T H Gladstone]	Clapham Gazette	1 Aug 1858
Mingrelia and Steam	The article describes the impact of the advent of steam navigation on the waterways in and around the Black Sea, Asia Minor.	Clapham Gazette	1 Sep 1858
The Chinese Treaty	The article describes the implications for commerce and the spread of Christianity of a peace treaty with China .	Clapham Gazette	1 Oct 1858
Infanticide in China?	The Rev. William C. Milne refutes Barrow's assertion that infanticide exists in China.	Clapham Gazette	1 Nov 1958
Ordination Service	The article reports on the ordination of Mr J. P. Ashton as a missionary to India and goes on to describe the religion, language and culture of India.	Clapham Gazette	1 Aug 1859
Chinese Barbers	Article about barbers in China.	Clapham Gazette	1 Aug 1859
The Chinese Tailor	Story about a tailor in Canton, China by Alexander Dumas.	Clapham Gazette	1 Sep 1859
Instinct and Intelligence	The differences between animals and humans. Includes comparisons of the intellect of men in civilised society and that of the indigenous tribes of Africa, Australia etc.	Clapham Gazette	1 Nov 1859
Lord Macaulay	Biog. of Thomas Macaulay, son of Zachary Macaulay, advocate for the abolition of slavery and member of the Clapham Sect.	Clapham Gazette	1 Feb 1860
The Church Missionary Society	Sermon given on the 26 February 1860 at Holy Trinity church, Clapham by the Rev Clement F. Cobb. The C M S's current involvement with Sierra Leone is described as is its historical connection with reference to Zachary Macaulay's efforts to train Sierra Leonese to preach/ evangelise.	Clapham Gazette	1 Mar 1860
British Orphan Asylum, Clapham Rise	A report of the anniversary of the founding of the British Orphan Asylum mentions that among the residents have been children from India, Australia and other British colonies.	Clapham Gazette	1 May 1860
Park Crescent Chapel	Report of the A G M of the Park Crescent Chapel Auxiliary of the London Missionary Society ; account of the missionaries in the field around the world and reports on their work in China and India.	Clapham Gazette	1 Jan 1861

Clapham Auxiliary of the London Missionary Society	Rev. J.B. Coles talks about India remarking on the vastness of the country and the amount of idols that the 'heathen' worship. Rev. W. Harbutt from the Samoan Islands, talks about the extent to which Christianity has spread in the South Pacific generally.	Clapham Gazette	1 May 1861
Nigger Melodists	Extract from Mr Driver's lecture on "Street Music". It praises the work of performers of 'nigger minstrelsy' who perform on London streets. Among the performers are mentioned Jim Crow, the "Ethiopian Serenaders", Banjo, Bones and Co. and Sam Blank all of whom were apparently white but dressed to look black. Mention is also made of the 'original street company of blacks'. It also includes a transcript of a conversation with Sam Blank, another, apparently well known, performer.	Clapham Gazette	1 Jun 1861
Fortune Telling	A report of the case of Selina Smith, a gypsy, who was charged at Wandsworth Police Court with obtaining a dress and 2 shillings from a Mrs. King of Wimbledon.	Clapham Gazette	1 Mar 1862
The Late War in China	Report by the Rev. Stephen Reed Cattley of an 'expedition against Peking' replete with comments on the character of the Chinese.	Clapham Gazette	1 Apr 1862
The Late Mr Pennington	An obituary of Mr Pennington, political economist, who was at one point engaged by the Treasury to regulate the currency of the West Indian Colonies.	Clapham Gazette	1 May 1862
Society for the Propagation of the Gospel:	The report of the Clapham meeting of this organisation; description of the fate of liberated slaves on the island of St. Helena; the author attributes the appearance of inferiority to the degrading treatment they received at the hands of their masters in the southern states of America.	Clapham Gazette	1 May 1862
Old Captain Brown	Concluding extract of a lecture given at the Clapham Literary and Scientific Institution includes an account of the protagonist's return to Kansas where he fell foul of the law having liberated a number of slaves.	Clapham Gazette	1 May 1862
Church Missionary Society	Report of the annual meeting of the Clapham Auxiliary of the Church Missionary society includes mention of the condition of the Sierra Leone Mission by the Rev. J. Graham and an account of the nature of Hinduism as practised in India by the Rev. Mr Pickford.	Clapham Gazette	1 May 1862
The Red Indian at "Garner"	A report of a lecture given by a Native American, the Rev. Mr Kelly: describes his experiences and those of his people at the hands of the 'pale faces'	Clapham Gazette	1 Feb 1863
Emancipation Meetings	Meeting at Exeter Hall of the Negro Emancipation Society; speakers: the Rev. Baptist Noel, the Rev. Newman Hall and Mr. T Hughes (*Tom Brown's School days*). Also of a meeting at St. James' Hall (same society?) 'a few days later'. Description of the mood and audience amongst whom are a number of black people.	Clapham Gazette	1 Mar 1863

A Day's Sight-seeing in Japan	A report of a lecture given by T. H. Howell Junior Esq. In *Clapham Literary and Scientific Institution* programme; description of the country, civilisation, government and people's characteristics.	Clapham Gazette	1 Apr 1863
The New York Riots	A report of riots by Irish and German immigrants in New York in protest at being made 'to fight for the negro'. The article describes the animosity felt by white working class immigrants for black people particularly in respect to the labour market.	Clapham Gazette	1 Aug 1863
Church Missionary Society	A report of the annual meeting of the Clapham auxiliary branch of this society. The Rev. Samuel Crowther, a native African clergyman, gives a talk which includes an autobiographical sketch, and an account of his work evangelising in West Africa.	Clapham Gazette	1 May 1864
Wandsworth District Board of Works	Summary report of the medical officers for Wandsworth District includes mention of the incidence of small pox among gypsies in an encampment on Streatham Common.	Clapham Gazette	1 Jun 1864
West Africa	Advices from the W. coast of Africa that trading has recommenced as the natives have been frightened into submission by Commodore Wilmott. Consequently, trade between the natives at Cape Palmas and the Liberian govt. was at an end.	S London Press	18 Feb 1865
Madagascar	The Queen of Madagascar is reported as stating: ' As long as I retain friendly relations with Queen Victoria, I shall be powerful.	S London Press	18 Feb 1865
Church Missionary Society	Rev. Mr. Cassell on the Society's work in Sierra Leone, mentioned the fact of slavery which 'prevailed even in England 100 years ago'. Granville Sharp and Jonathon Strong case were also referred to.	S London Press	25 Feb 1865
Dunn's Lecture Hall, Newington Causeway	A grand evening concert, featuring amongst others, Messrs. Newman & Bromley (niggers)…who added much to the amusement	S London Press	25 Feb 1865
Unlawful nigger entertainment	Rotherhithe publican – David Laurence of the Royal Standard – was prosecuted for unlicensed entertainment (the singing of niggers with banjos and bones).	S London Press	25 Feb 1865
Local amusements	Southern Minstrels at the Deptford Institute	S London Press	4 Mar 1865
Local amusements	In Dundee, Emma Billett (married to a negro lecturer named Johnstone) was sentenced to 14 days imprisonment for theft	S London Press	11 Mar 1865
Murder on the High Seas	John Christopher Bennett (22) was indicted for the murder of John West, a man of colour, who was a seaman on board the British ship Raymond at Liverpool Assizes. Guilty of manslaughter and sentenced to 15 years .	S London Press	1 Apr 1865

District news	An address to the Surrey Chapel on Slavery by Edward Baines M.P. and Reverend Crammond Kennedy of New York. A collection was made for the Freedmen's Relief Assoc. (To feed clothe and educate the emancipated)	S London Press	8 Apr 1865
Local amusements	Zoilffmerddo Minstrels at Lammas Hall Battersea. (White practitioners of minstrelsy)	S London Press	15 Apr 1865
Hottentot Venus	A Hottentot Venus ('…upon whose claims to the title it would of course be unfair to comment') was displayed at Knot Hill Fair in Manchester	S London Press	22 Apr 1865
A preacher turned pugilist	William Wiliams a preacher on American slavery was charged with vagrancy in Dundee	S London Press	10 Jun 1865
Local amusements	The Real Alabama Minstrels are scheduled to appear at the Victoria Theatre	S London Press	17 Jun 1865
Local amusements	The Real Alabama Minstrels perform the drama 'Down South' at the Victoria Theatre	S London Press	24 Jun 1865
Strong-minded American Woman	Announcing the marriage of Ann Dickerson (a white orator) to Frederick Douglas Jnr in New York. *According to the New York correspondent of the Morning Herald*	S London Press	1 July 1865
A Negro Lecturer and his Printer	A man of colour named Jackson (a lecturer on slavery) was awarded 30s. damages for destroyed bills and placards printed erroneously by a Mr. Ainsworthy of Piccadilly, Manchester	S London Press	1 July 1865
Church Missionary Society	Report of the annual meeting of the Clapham Auxiliary branch of this society in which the Rev. T. J. Gaster and the Rev. T. Y. Darling describe their missionary experience in India.	Clapham Gazette	1 July 1865
A Southwark MP	A biographical account of Henry Thornton including a description of his involvement with the Clapham Sect.	Clapham Gazette	1 July 1865
London Amusements	Appearing at the Alhambra Music Hall in Shoreditch – Lewis and Gardiner, 'negro delineators'.	S London Press	22 July 1865
Queen of the Sandwich Isles	Queen Emma of the Sandwich Isles visited Christ Church, Clapham. A collection was made for the Hawaiian Mission ; sermon preached by Queen Emma's own chaplain, Rev. W. Hoapili	S London Press	12 Aug 1865
A faithless and brutal husband	John Folks Fenton a 'nigger' musician is committed to 21 days hard labour for violent assault upon his wife.	S London Press	12 Aug 1865
London Amusements	'Mr. Ira Aldridge, a negro tragedian is the latest sensation in the theatrical world of London. He plays the Moor in Othello at the Haymarket and is pronounced by the critics as very good. For lack of space we defer notice of this 'real' black.	S London Press	26 Aug 1865

What will be done with the negro?	Editorial criticising racial policies in the United States	S London Press	2 Sep 1865
Visit of a Chinese Giant	A reception was held at the Manor House, Newington for Chang the Chinese giant. The reception '…seems to have given anything but satisfaction to a large number of inhabitants of the district and to some connected with the hospital.'	S London Press	9 Sep 1865
London Amusements	Chang, the 8ft. tall giant of Fychou is appearing at the Egyptian Hall, Piccadilly.	S London Press	30 Sep 1865
Home and Foreign News	Hannibal Hamilton, King of the Tumut tribe died on the 5th August. The race of Australian aborigines known as the Doomut or Toomut Blacks is fast becoming extinct.	S London Press	28 Oct 1865
Mr Hughes, MP on the freed men of America	The Rev Sella Martin, a negro who had been a slave, entered into minute details as to the present condition and prospects of the coloured race during a public meeting at Hanover Chapel, Peckham on behalf of the 4 million freedmen of the United States.	S London Press	4 Nov 1865
Insurrection	It is announced that an insurrection has broken out in the portion of Jamaica. The governor had made an urgent appeal for assistance to Gen. Doyle, the military commander. Admiral Hope immediately set sail in his flagship, the *Duncan*, with a battalion of the 17th Regiment and a second vessel was to follow immediately. The cause or extent of the outbreak is unknown.	S London Press	4 Nov 1865
Negro Rebellion	An outline of the latest reports from Jamaica	S London Press	18 Nov 1865
Home and foreign news	More Jamaican reports	S London Press	18 Nov 1865
Frightful atrocities by the negroes	Opinions and anecdotes of the rebellion from the New York Daily News	S London Press	18 Nov 1865
Race and Religion	Lecture by the Rev. T. J. Gaster "to apply the results of recent enquiries into Race and Language to the order in which Christianity was received by different races in Apostolic times, and thence to infer the probable order in which Christianity would be received by the representatives of those races now living in North India".	Clapham Gazette	1 Dec 1865
The Jamaica Outbreak	Sermon delivered by Rev. Baldwin Brown "on the necessity of a searching enquiry into the late affair in Jamaica".	Clapham Gazette	1 Dec 1865
Atrocities in Jamaica	An editorial condemnation of the behaviour of British policy in Jamaica	S London Press	2 Dec 1865
Massacres in Jamaica	A public meeting at Lambeth Baths attended by upwards of 1,000 people, calling for an inquiry into the massacres.	S London Press	2 Dec 1865

Our Civilisation	An editorial condemnation of the behaviour of British policy in Jamaica	S London Press	9 Dec 1865
Marriages	17th Nov 1865 at Grenwich, Sidi Ali, son of Sidi Yud Rafael Salem Ali, Chieftan of the tribe of Ali, Lwr. Abysinnia to Mary A.E.A.H.G Sinibaldi, only daughter of Signor Louis Sinibaldi of Greenwich	S London Press	9 Dec 1865
Eyewitness on affairs in Jamaica	Rev. Alfred Bourne, of Clapham, recently returned from Jamaica, tells of his experience.	S London Press	16 Dec 1865
The Jamaica Insurrection	A report into the different ways in which the insurrection in Jamaica had been reported by the press.	Clapham Gazette	1 Jan 1866
General News	On 19th Nov, the natives of New Calabar made a raid on the Brass men through Calabar Creek and returned on the 23rd of November with 37 prisoners. On 24th Nov great play was held in Calabar town and all the prisoners were killed and eaten. After death the bodies were cut up and divided amongst the chiefs according to the number taken by each war canoe. Trade was in consequence stopped.	S London Press	13 Jan 1866
Advertisement	Smith and Wilson, described as 'Sensation Blacks' were performing at Gatti's Music Hall Westminster Bridge Road	S London Press	13 Jan 1866
Local Entertainments	Listed as performing at Gatti's Music Hall are 'two darkies full of humour, (presumably Smith and Wilson).	S London Press	13 Jan 1866
A Giant's tea-party	A tea party and soiree were given at the Egyptian rooms, Piccadilly by the wife of Chang the Chinese giant (from Fychou).	S London Press	20 Jan 1866
17 Years among the Blacks	The death of James Merrill was announced in Port Davison, Australia. He had lived amongst the aborigines for 17 years.	S London Press	27 Jan 1866
Lambeth News	Discussion on the Jamaican question at the Waterloo Road (Wesleyan) Young Men's Society	S London Press	6 Jan 1866
The Jamaica Outbreak	A Baptist Missionary Society meeting was held at the Metropolitan Tabernacle to adopt an address of sympathy to the ministers and missionaries connected with the society in Jamaica	S London Press	3 Feb 1866
Surrey Chapel	A lecture by Youhannah el Karem on the 'Manners and Customs of the East'	S London Press	17 Feb 1866
Local Amusements	Lee's Minstrels – the coloured gentlemen massed under this title gave the first of a series of Saturday evening performances in the Lecture Hall, Hill St. Peckham.	S London Press	17 Feb 1866

Society for the Propagation of the Gospel	Rev. H. Rowley gives an account of his experiences as companion of Bishop Mackenzie when forming part of the Universities' mission to central Africa. Includes remarks on the character and customs of the indigenous population and on the practice of slavery.	Clapham Gazette	1 Mar 1866
The Casuals again	Anthony Charles Lewis, a man of colour, and George Turner were committed to 21 days hard labour for misbehaving at the casual ward of Lambeth workhouse	S London Press	3 Mar 1866
Aid for the negro	A meeting of the Freedmen's Aid Society at Camberwell Hall, Grove Lane to hail the abolition of slavery in the United States. A collection was taken	S London Press	10 Mar 1866
Church Missionary Society	A report of the Clapham Association in connection with this society in which the Rev. J. J. Jones describes the work of the society in Ceylon.	Clapham Gazette	1 Jun 1866
London Amusements	A negro actor, Mr. Morgan Smith, a native of Philadelphia whose colour has been a bar to his appearing in any theatre in his own country is about to appear on the English stage	S London Press	7 July 1866
General News	'The other morning at 2 o'clock, a negro melodist living in St. Clement's Lane went onto the parapet of the house to smoke his pipe according to his wont before going to bed when he fell into the street below and was killed	S London Press	14 July 1866
London Amusements 'Blind Tom'	A blind 18 year old African-American piano prodigy appears at the Egyptian Rooms prior to a tour of the provinces. Although described as 'half-idiotic', his pianoforte style is reported to have been 'perfect and very brilliant'.	S London Press	4 Aug 1866
A Woman of Colour	Mary Ann Witherby was charged with wounding PC Dearling wit the intention of causing grievous bodily harm.	S London Press	15 Sep 1866
Gypsy Life	A report of a case brought before Wandsworth Police Court which reveals something about gypsy life in the district.	Clapham Gazette	1 Dec 1866
Surrey Sessions – A Black Case	James Cooley, 20, a man of colour, was indicted for stealing a gold watch and chain of the value of £6, the property of James Adams, landlord of the King's Arms, Wandsworth	S London Press	5 Jan 1867
Church Missionary Society	A report of a meeting of this society in which Archdeacon Hunter describes the life style of the native Americans in his diocese of Rupert's Land.	Clapham Gazette	1 May 1867
London Missionary Society	A report of a meeting of the Clapham Auxiliary of this society in which the work of the society is described in progress in South America and the West Indies.	Clapham Gazette	1 May 1867
Suicide of a Licensed Victualler	Report of the suicide of Mr George Colman of the Bull's Head Inn, Clapham Old Town, who was under the delusion that gypsies were going to kill him	Clapham Gazette	1 Jun 1867

Church Missionary Society	AGM describes work in Africa: "Mr Girdlestone held in his hand the first charge of the first bishop of western Africa delivered on the banks of the river during 1866 to his black clergy....It was in very truth a testimony of the fact that the black man could think and speak as we ourselves" with account of work in India.	Clapham Gazette	1 Jul 1867
Suicide of a Parsee Youth	Rosstunjee Burzorjee, the 16 year old son of a Parsee merchant, is reported to have committed suicide at Putney Railway station on 12 October 1867	Clapham Gazette	1 Nov 1867
Abyssinian Expedition	A report on a debate in the House of Commons concerning the recently declared war with Abyssinia.	Clapham Gazette	1 Dec 1867
Local Police News	'A nigger named Victory was committed for trial charged with robbing a Brighton gentleman of his gold watch in Borough High St.	S London Press	25 Jan 1868
Entertainment at Clapham Hall	Report of an evening of entertainment at Clapham Hall, 14 Jan 1868, in which minstrels performed and an oration about the distinction between 'white niggers' and 'black niggers' took place.	Clapham Gazette	1 Feb 1868
Surrey Sessions – A Bloodless Victory	'A negro named Thomas Victory was charged with stealing a watch and guard, the property of Mr. H.D. Richards, Lower Rd Lambeth. The prosecutor was coming down Blackman St...when somebody jostled up against him sharply. On recovering his balance he missed his watch and followed the man, whom he lost sight of for a moment, but almost immediately found prisoner in the arms of a policeman. The night being dark he couldn't identify the man. Police constable 215M said that he stopped the prisoner, who immediately exclaimed, " I ain't got the watch". Prisoner said he was going to Wandsworth and as it came on raining was running to keep himself warm when the policeman cried "Hey!" and stopped him. The jury gave prisoner the benefit of the dubious identity and acquitted him.	S London Press	8 Feb 1868
The Story of the Freed Negress	Mrs Jacobs, an ex-slave delivers an address at Newton House, Kensington of her experiences in Virginia before and after the American Civil War.	S London Press	15 Feb 1868
Atrocious Outrage by a Nigger	William Spillon, an attendant at a wild beast show, was committed for six months with hard labour for an assault with a pitchfork which wounded Henry Brodey ,7.	S London Press	22 Feb 1868
Clapham Auxiliary Bible Society	At the meeting of the 55th anniversary of this society the Rev. Aubrey C. Price talked about the justification for war with Abyssinia and the Rev. W. Muirhead talked about the people of China and their habits.	Clapham Gazette	1 Jun 1868
Church Missionary Society	Report of the annual meeting of this society at which the Rev. Henry Townsend, missionary from Abbeokuta, West Africa, talks about his experiences spreading the gospel there	Clapham Gazette	1 Jul 1868
Crystal Palace	Monday to Friday – 1s – Performances each day by the amazing Beni Zoug-Zoug Arabs.	S London Press	25 Jul 1868

General Law & Police – A Negro who had a tough head and a tender heart.	At the Bury Petty Sessions Martin Grimes was charged with having cut and wounded John Henry Davis, a negro, by striking him on the head with a poker which inflicted a wound one inch deep. Davis pleaded for his assaulter to be allowed to go unpunished, claiming that a state of drunkenness had been the cause of the attack. Assailant was required to pay 14s. or to be imprisoned for 14 days.	S London Press	15 Aug 1868
Shocking Barbarities Aboard Ship	At the Liverpool Assizes the captain and 2nd mate of the ship *Lydia* were found guilty on the charge of exercising revolting cruelties towards the coloured seamen, Charles Fuller, Robert Williams, Richard Martin and Joseph Campbell. The Captain (Scovill) and the 2nd mate (Carroll), were sentenced to two and one years imprisonment with hard labour apiece.	S London Press	29 Aug 1868
Amateur Negro Entertainment	Report of a performance of the "CCC Amateur Negro Minstrels" at Clapham Hall on 28 Jan 1869 including the performers Bones and Pompey	Clapham Gazette	1 Feb 1869
Church Missionary Society	AGM, the Rev. Harding Dixon refutes the contention that "the money spent in the work of preaching the gospel to the heathen was wasted, heathenism being so engrafted on the minds of the people that it can not be eradicated" by describing his experiences as a missionary in Tinnevelly, southern India.	Clapham Gazette	1 Jul 1869
Royal Original Christie Minstrels	A report of a musical evening at Clapham Hall on 8 June 1869 where the "Royal Original Christie Minstrels" played.	Clapham Gazette	1 Jul 1869
Lectures at Wandsworth Rd.	Report of a lecture given at the Commercial schools by the Rev. J. McCarthy, Minister of St Saviour's, Battersea Park entitled "Races and Places in the Punjab".	Clapham Gazette	1 Apr 1870
British and Foreign Bible Society	Annual meeting of this society in which their missionary work in a number of countries. Mention is also made of "that remarkable Hindoo who is now in London".	Clapham Gazette	1 Jun 1870
Church Missionary Society	A report of a meeting held in connection with this society on 19 May 1870 in which the Rev. A. E. Moule spoke of his experiences as a missionary in China.	Clapham Gazette	1 Jun 1870
Church Missionary Society	An annual report of the Clapham Association of this society in which the Rev. T. R. Wade describes his experiences as a missionary in Northern India.	Clapham Gazette	1 Jul 1870
Singular Charge of Conspiracy	A report of a case of conspiracy at Wandsworth Police Court in which a "dark-haired gypsy girl" is accused of conspiracy to defraud.	Clapham Gazette	1 Oct 1870
Royal Aboriginal Minstrels	A report of an evening of entertainment held at Clapham Hall on 4 November 1870 in which "The Royal Aboriginal Minstrels" 'garbed after the fashion of negro minstrels' performed. The names of the performers are included.	Clapham Gazette	1 Dec 1870

Colonial and Continental Church Society	The Rev. E. Forbes at a meeting on December 14 1870 described activities of society in Newfoundland; including groups who have benefited from this society's activities including: 'French Settlers', 'the coloured population' and 'Red Indians'.	Clapham Gazette	1 Jan 1871
Course of Lectures at Wandsworth	The Rev. Arthur E. Moule gave a lecture at the Commercial school entitled "China in Peace and War" on 3 February 1871.	Clapham Gazette	1 Mar 1871
British and Foreign Bible Society	AGM of Clapham auxiliary; report of this meeting held on April 18 1871 in which missionary work in Africa is described.	Clapham Gazette	1 May 1871
Church Missionary Society	A report of the annual meeting of the Clapham Association of this society held on 9 June 1871 in which missionary work in India is described.	Clapham Gazette	1 Jul 1871
The new expedition to Central Africa	Letters received from Stanley "without the powerful assistance of Mtesa, King of Uganda he would not have reached the lakes Victoria and Albert Nyanza.", attacks by 'natives', etc..	At Home and Abroad	Sep 1876
Religious Tract Society.	A foreign grants: among many others: Syria £18; Punjab £100; Jamaica £3, Demerara £1; Durban £1, Lagos £5	At Home and Abroad	Sep 1876
'Wilberforce' Band of Hope	quarterly tea meeting and entertainment, St Mary, Lambeth; featuring the dialogue 'Contended Tom' by Masters W. and H. Davies	Westminster and Lambeth Gazette	11 Feb 1882
Grosvenor Hall	Thursday evening a concert by 'The Wandering Minstrels' (prob. white)	Westminster and Lambeth Gazette	11 Feb 1882
St. Stephen's (Westminster)	On Saturday last the club minstrels gave their second performance (prob. white)	Westminster and Lambeth Gazette	18 Feb 1882
Westminster Democratic Club: 'Our Colonies'	'Mr. C. Pfoundes lectured to a crowded audience, on "Our Colonies, their value, with hints on Emigration" . Chinese cheap labour is competition for the English colonial emigrants who should be given preference	Westminster and Lambeth Gazette	31 Mar 1882
The 'Free Library', Kennington Lane	arts exhibition was visited on Sunday evening by at least 1,015 persons/ mentions Cetewayo's, (king of the Zulu) visit and 'a soul-stirring picture by De Neuville, 'The Defence of Rorke's Drift. It was pleasant to hear an intelligent artizan describing to his boys how the gallant Lieutenant Chard and his little garrison of 104 men held their frail camp against a host of Zulus, …'	Westminster and Lambeth Gazette	19 Aug 1882
Big Ben's Telephone	meeting held at Westminster Palace Hotel on Monday 'thanking Mr Saul Solomon of Cape Town for his services on behalf of the natives.'	Westminster and Lambeth Gazette	11 Nov 1882
no title	'The Indian contingent were received at Westminster Abbey by the Dean on Wednesday. They were shown the grave of Lord Laurence, and other memorials.'	Westminster and Lambeth Gazette	18 Nov 1882

Current Notes	Thomas Smith, labourer, charged with assaulting John Acca, a Chinaman, of Great Peter Street, and Walter Bennet with assaulting John's daughter, Sarah. Acca came to England poor, but now owns property 'acquired by thrift and industry' in Westminster.	Westminster and Lambeth Gazette	16 Dec 1882
The Missing Link	'M. Farinis curious importation from Siam continues to excite considerable curiosity among visitors to the Royal Aquarium': Krao, a ca. six year old 'child of a tribe of hairy peoples, speaks little English and 'will not hear of going back to her country where she says there are no beds'.	Westminster and Lambeth Gazette	20 Jan 1883
Miss Anthony in Lambeth	'one of the most agreeable at homes of the season': suffragette and anti-slavery agitator from the United States [see also Editorial]	Westminster and Lambeth Gazette	23 Jun 1883
Balloon Society	lecture at Royal Aquarium 22 June 'Madagascar, its land and people' by Rev. C.J. Woodward [displays very negative views on people: e.g. lying, drunkenness, cheating, are prevalent, etc].	Westminster and Lambeth Gazette	30 Jun 1883
Leaflets for Ladies .	mentions meeting a young Chinese gentlemen, student at the Royal Naval College, who 'spoke English perfectly and gave me the impression of much ability'. Mentions anti-Chinese legislation in California.	Westminster and Lambeth Gazette	7 Jul 1883
A Dark, Disorderly Barrister	'Mr Christian F. Cole, described as a barrister, and giving an address in Millman-Lane, was fined 40 s. at Bow-street, for being very drunk and disorderly in Bedford-row on Tuesday night. He is a man of colour, and is said to have been very abusive to the policeman who took him into custody. The magistrate administered a severe censure.'	Westminster and Lambeth Gazette	7 Jul 1883
A Romantic Story	Mr Tahrir Udin Ahmed, Indian gentlemen and student got conned by a young lady who disappeared with some of his jewellery	Westminster and Lambeth Gazette	18 Aug 1883
The 'Romantic Story'	Ms Blanche Coulton was acquitted – she had been charged with stealing three rings from Mr Tahrir Udin Ahmed	Westminster and Lambeth Gazette	25 Aug 1883
The Balloon Society	Colonel Parker-Gillmore read paper on 'the Transvaal and its boundaries'. Favours indirect rule for the 'natives'. Has 'never found better workers than in the Zulu race, and though their skins were black their hearts were whiter than many Englishmen's.'	Westminster and Lambeth Gazette	27 Oct 1883
Balloon Society	South Africa lecture, on Transvaal. Reference to race relations and abolitionists	Westminster and Lambeth Gazette	10 Nov 1883
Eccleston Conference Hall	on Wednesday evening a *Conversazione* was held to 'bid farewell to a number of missionaries. Addresses were held by among others, 'an African lad, Mavungi.'	Westminster and Lambeth Gazette	29 Mar 1884

Elephant and Castle Theatre	After a short but successful run 'Uncle Tom's Cabin' will be withdrawn in favour of ' The Watercress Girl' a drama invested with a certain amount of local interest…	Westminster and Lambeth Gazette	30 Aug 1884
no title;	Mr E.G. Ravenstein, of Brixton, read a paper before the British Association, at Montreal, on Exploration in Africa before the 17th century.	Westminster and Lambeth Gazette	30 Aug 1884
The Pigmies at the Aquarium	'N'co N'qui (a chief), his wife 'N'Arbecy, and 3 others from the Kalahari dessert, South Africa, are being exhibited as Mr Farini's "African Pigmies", or "Dwarf Earthmen". Mentions that "5 of the best specimen" managed to escape their capturer on the way to the Cape. "From all the accounts it seems to be a shockingly cruel, treacherous and ferocious little race".	Westminster and Lambeth Gazette	20 Sep 1884
St. Luke's Nightingale Lane	Bishop of Minnesota on the positive effects of missionary work, on the former cannibals in Polynesia. It is a wonderful thing that God gave America to the Anglo-Saxon race before all others….	Westminster and Lambeth Gazette	29 Nov 1884
Brixton Liberal Club Brixton Hall	'Mr Geo. Robertson lent a very interesting collection of Zulu articles, including weapons and domestic utensils. An ill-informed description of Zulu's headrests and marriage follows	Westminster and Lambeth Gazette	10 Jan 1885
Leaflets for Ladies/ Female Education in India	Paper read by Mancherjee M. Bhownagree, 'a Parsee who came to this country to study law bringing his sister with him to receive an English education'. Abstract of the paper (historical outline of education for women) and discussion follows. Mr Thornton puts emphasis on medical education, hospitals 'not only places of healing, but also temples of conciliation, and schools of sympathy between the different races'.	Westminster and Lambeth Gazette	21 Mar 1885
Soudan Expedition	The Admiralty and War Office have passed orders to Messrs Merryweather & Sons, of Greenwich and Long Acre, for five portable steam pumping engines, and several miles of hose piping, for water supply purposes in the Soudan.	Westminster and Lambeth Gazette	21 Mar 1885
Princess Louise Home and the Jubilee Singers	The Fisk University Jubilee Singers gave a concert at *Grosvenor House* on behalf of the Home for Young Girls, and under the patronage of her Royal Highness Princess Louise (she arrived a little late and left a little early though….). Article is very positive about the group and the music, and addresses the context of gospel and slavery. Mentions that they had performed 'Steal away to Jesus' before the German Kaiser. Mr. F.J. Loudin, the director gave a speech explaining the fundraising mission for Fisk University and the need for education for 4 ½ million of people who had suffered slavery. Miss W. A. Benchley on the piano.	Westminster and Lambeth Gazette	24 Apr 1885

84

no title,	It will astonish those not well up in Chinese customs to learn that when a Chinese gentleman was asked about what the Magistrate at Marlborough Street Court called ' a half educated drunken lad' he was asked by the chief clerk 'whether he wanted to be sworn on a saucer or to make an affirmation.' He, however, preferred to take the oath in the usual way upon the Bible.	Westminster and Lambeth Gazette	4 Jul 1885
Big Ben's Telephone	Mr E. Schilling is now providing services of Sacred Songs, in the Beresford Assembly Rooms. Last Sunday, the solos, hymns, and other sacred pieces were ably rendered by a small troupe of Freed Slaves from the Southern States. An interesting address was also given [by] Miss R. White, a coloured lady of the troupe.	Westminster and Lambeth Gazette	11 Jul 1885
Albert Palace, Battersea	As part of the bank holiday entertainment programme, Hadji Ali Achmed's Bedouin Arabs perform.	Westminster and Lambeth Gazette	1 Aug 1885
Albert Palace, Battersea	25,000 people entered on Monday to see the amusement, among them Hadji Ali Achmed's Bedouin Arabs perform.	Westminster and Lambeth Gazette	8 Aug 1885
The Royal Aquarium	As one of the attractions 'Messrs. Field and Hansom, a clever and amusing couple of nigger entertainers' are listed.	Westminster and Lambeth Gazette	8 Aug 1885
An Indian Village at the Albert Palace	Fifty skilled artists and entertainers from India will demonstrate wood carving, metal work, weaving, dance, snake charming, etc. They are expected to arrive at the end of the months.	Westminster and Lambeth Gazette	17 Oct 1885
Moffat Institute. Exhibition.	Miss Moffat, the daughter of the late missionary, sent a 'large and interesting collection of curiosities collected by her father in central Africa.	Westminster and Lambeth Gazette	17 Oct 1885
National Liberal Club	Mr Lal Mohun Ghose on "What should be the chief objects of the proposed enquiry into the government of India?" at weekly discussion last Wednesday.	Westminster and Lambeth Gazette	27 Mar 1886
Science at the 'Vic'	lecture on social life in India, incl. superstition, etc.	Westminster and Lambeth Gazette	8 May 1886
King Cetewayo's Niece in Lambeth	the case of Princess Azahmglona was heard at Lambeth Police Court: after her uncle's and father's capture, she came to Britain and together with 'others of her own race' she had arranged to give certain entertainments, e.g. war dances. She joined a troupe performing Uncle Tom's Cabin, had also made an arrangement to perform in London. She borrowed £2 to get from Cardiff to London, where she was left destitute due to cancellation by the agent. She however was engaged to perform now at the Royal Victoria Hall, Waterloo Road. The magistrate gave her 'some assistance'.	Westminster and Lambeth Gazette	15 May 1886

Prize Day at Charing Cross Medical School	Mr Pisam has won the first prize on the Indian list.	Westminster and Lambeth Gazette	12 Jun 1886
Warner's Safe Cure	advert for patent medicine for the "kidneys, liver and urinary organs" showing image of an African male collecting herbs into a basket on his back	Westminster and Lambeth Gazette	19 Jun 1886
A Facetious 'Darkey'	"At Marlborough – street Police Court a coloured man who gave the name of 'Robert the Devil' was charged with being drunk and disorderly." incident happened at Oxford Street where he was surrounded by a large crowd and using 'filthy' language. He had been before the court many times.	Westminster and Lambeth Gazette	25 Oct 1886
Cruelty to a dog	Kama Dingero, a Japanese employed at the Japanese Village, summoned for cruelty to a dog.	Westminster and Lambeth Gazette	16 Oct 1886
Mr Ravenstein's New Geographical Work	Mr Ravenstein from the Brixton Liberal Club, is at present working on maps on Western Equatorial Africa on 21 sheets, and a descriptive handbook using facts by over 3,300 explorers, writers, missionaries and scientific investigators.	Westminster and Lambeth Gazette	15 Jan 1887
Science at the 'Vic'	lecture on 'The people of India' by Hilliard Atteridge	Westminster and Lambeth Gazette	30 Apr 1887
Pennsylvania Jubilee Singers	On Sunday afternoon last, the above choir gave some excellent selections in the Christ Church, Lambeth.	Westminster and Lambeth Gazette	14 May 1887
Ismail Pacha [Pasha]	Ismail Pasha: This well known Egyptian arrived at Charing Cross station on Sunday afternoon last by the mail train from Paris.	Westminster and Lambeth Gazette	14 May 1887
National Temperance League	lecture by Rev. G. Gregson on drink in Bengal, attended by Mr Lahmoun Ghose, a native Hindoo, barrister-at-law	Westminster and Lambeth Gazette	21 May 1887
Garden Party at Lambeth Palace	on Saturday afternoon, among the guests: the United States Minister and Mrs. Phelps, the Queen Kapiolani of Hawaii and the Princess Lilinokalani.	Westminster and Lambeth Gazette	2 July 1887
The Church of England Temperance Society.	A bazaar was opened by the Duchess at the Duke of Wellington's Riding School on Tuesday. It had been opened on Tuesday [twice?] by Her Majesty Queen Kapiolani of Hawaii, accompanied by Her Royal Highness the Princess Lilinokalani and suite.	Westminster and Lambeth Gazette	2 July 1887
St. George's (Hanover Square) Union	meeting of board at vestry: The Three Hindooes. Three Hindoos at the Fulham workhouse, are landowners from Goojerat. After a dispute over land, and unsuccessful court case in Punjaub, they were advised to put their case before the Privy Council. .	Westminster and Lambeth Gazette	23 July 1887

St. George's (Hanover Square) Union	meeting of board of Guardians at vestry: The Three Hindooes. A letter was read from the Local Government Board, enclosing an emigration order, authorising the expenditure by the Guardians of a sum not exceeding £20 for the emigration to India of the three Hindoos, named Mehran Buse, Mahomed Yar, and Katubudden.	Westminster and Lambeth Gazette	30 July 1887
St. George's (Hanover Square) Union	meeting of board at vestry: The Three Hindooes. Three Hindoos at the Fulham workhouse, are landowners from Goojerat. After a dispute over land, and unsuccessful court case in Punjaub, they were advised to put their case before the Privy Council. However they lost all their money and were left without means. It was suggested to send them back at a cost of £16. Adopted.	Westminster and Lambeth Gazette	13 July 1887
St. George's (Hanover Square) Union	meeting of board of Guardians: The Three Hindoos/ Local Government Board forwarding extract of letters from the India Office. Viscount Cross was unable to depart from the established practice of the India Office which was not accepting any responsibility as to providing for such persons or for sending them back to India. Since they are paupers they are entitled to relief under the ordinary law of England. As regards the general question an committee was appointed with representatives of the Colonial Office and the Local Government Board to discuss position of natives of India and other people from the East becoming destitute in this country.	Westminster and Lambeth Gazette	13 Aug 1887
St. James Vestry. Foreign Prostitutes	The Parliamentary Bill's Committee recommended that " That the Home Secretary be requested to initiate legislation with a view to confirming upon Courts of Summary Jurisdiction in the metropolis, power to require foreign prostitutes convicted of loitering in the streets for the purpose of prostitution or soliciting, to return to their own country upon pain of imprisonment or heavy fine if they repeat the offence in the metropolis."	Westminster and Lambeth Gazette	1 Oct 1887
St George's (Hanover Square)	A Mr R.G. Webster said that one of the main causes for destitution in the metropolis was that destitute aliens were allowed to flow in – taking work away…	Westminster and Lambeth Gazette	29 Oct 1887
Current Notes	A deputation from the Japanese village appeared at Westminster Police Court. They had been discharged at a weeks notice and were left destitute, their passage money having been refused. Magistrate suggested to sue the employer in the County Court.	Westminster and Lambeth Gazette	29 Oct 1887
Sir J. Lubbock at the Victoria Hall	before a large audience, he gave a very "entertaining" lecture on the customs and ideas of savages	Westminster and Lambeth Gazette	26 Nov 1887
Fighting the Foreigner	A Japanese Lady , Owakerson, sued the Japanese Village organisers for not covering her return journey, due to changes in management. She was won the case, and was given £50.	Westminster and Lambeth Gazette	17 Dec 1887

Magpie Minstrels	The Magpie Minstrels, an 'amateur negro troup' gave an entertainment at the Drill Hall, Upper Kennington, in aid of the Montrose Drum and Fife band. They performed songs and ballads. Messrs. H.F. Godfrey, Dr. S. Albyn, J.A. Mason, H.T. Hall, Bishop, Chapman-Herring, Laing, and Master Walder.	Westminster and Lambeth Gazette	24 Dec 1887
Church Mission Services in Lambeth	Anniversary sermons held by Rev. T.R. Wade, a missionary from Punjaub. Gives short account of history of the Society, and especially figures of 'native clergy'; 32 negroes, 149 Hindus, Singalese, etc. and Chinese, 25 new Zealanders. There is one native bishop on the Niger Mission. On Monday evening a lecture was delivered on East Africa: mentions that the slave trade is still going on.	Westminster and Lambeth Gazette	17 Mar 1888
Englishmen Taught by Men of Colour	Meeting of the Lambeth branch of the Church of England Temperance Society, the following 'native' gentlemen were present: Mr Jehangu Pestonji (of Bombay), Mr Odambuko Sapard (of Africa) and Mr Chowy Nurthin (of Madras) spoke on the topic.	Westminster and Lambeth Gazette	12 May 1888
Egyptian Joseph	On Wednesday at Westminster Police Court, Joseph Laci, an Egyptian describing himself as an artists model, was charged with assaulting his son. The son was bleeding from wound on the head and told the landlady that his father had hit him with a boot.	Westminster and Lambeth Gazette	26 May 1888
Gypsies	Article on prejudice against Gypsies and their cultural background.	Westminster and Lambeth Gazette	30 Jun 1888
A Jamaica Pastor at Boro' Road Chapel	Mr F.E. Marston, a coloured man from Jamaica, occupied pulpit. He is completing his study of the ministry to later on return to Jamaica.	Westminster and Lambeth Gazette	25 Aug 1888
George Street Mission, Lambeth Walk	The Jubilee Singers gave an evening of sacred songs. Mr C. Hutchinson (of Brixton) referred 'very touchingly to the poor slaves in Africa, and urging upon all present to use their personal influence in doing what they could to aid their coloured brethren in distant lands, and to set a noble example at home.' The spacious hall was well filled…	Westminster and Lambeth Gazette	10 Nov 1888
Castle Lane Youth's Institute	at the 5th annual new year's reception Tableaux Vivants were shown, among them 'The Slave Mart'	Westminster and Lambeth Gazette	19 Jan 1889
Arrangements at the Victoria Hall	on the 12th of February Commander Cameron will give lecture on 'Africa and the horrors of the slave trade'	Westminster and Lambeth Gazette	2 Feb 1889
Royal Victoria Hall	On the 12th instant Commander Cameron C.B., R.N., (the first white man who crossed tropical Africa from East to West) would lecture on Africa, the horrors of the slave trade and the liquor traffic with the native races.	Westminster and Lambeth Gazette	9 Feb 1889

Big Ben's Telephone	The question of slavery in relation to trade in Africa will be discussed at the meeting of the Society of Arts, on Tuesday next. Commander Cameron will read a paper.	Westminster and Lambeth Gazette	16 Feb 1889
Mr Samuel Brandram at Brixton Hall	Peformance included 'The Last Shot'… " a stirring and pathetic tale of the Indian Mutiny, he threw wonderful force and spirit, at the same time drawing the thin line between the reciter and the actor."	Westminster and Lambeth Gazette	6 Feb 1889
Olla Podrida	The heiress to the throne of Hawaii is coming to England to complete her education. She is Princess Victoria Kauitani, and is fourteen years of age.	Westminster and Lambeth Gazette	4 May 1889
London School of Medicine for women	winter season opening Tuesday last with 'the usual gathering', among others: Miss Cornelia Sorabji, Rukhmabai, Mr Motiiram S. Advani, and two Indian gentlemen.	Westminster and Lambeth Gazette	5 Oct 1889
Big Ben's Telephone	Miss Colenso will lecture at the National Liberal Club next Tuesday evening on the Zulu question, Miss Colenso being an ardent advocate of the rights of native races. Ladies are invited to be present.	Westminster and Lambeth Gazette	12 Apr 1890
Whitsuntide Amusements	mentions the Australian funambulist [a rope dancer] Ella Zuila in the same sentence as the Stanley and Livingstone baboons and the kangaroo baby.	Westminster and Lambeth Gazette	31 May 1890
Kenington Liberal Association	quarterly meeting at the 'Wheasheaf', South Lambeth Road, on Friday, the 30th ult.. Mr Surendra Nath Banerjee, (delegate from the Indian National Congress, Principal of Ripol College, Calcutta, Presidency Magistrate, and Municipal Commissioner of Calcutta), and Mr R.N. Mudholkar, L.C.B., B.A., and Mr V.M. Joshi were present.; addressed the meeting on representative government,	Westminster and Lambeth Gazette	7 Jun 1890
National Indian Association	AGM held at the Westminster Palace Hotel, on Wednesday, under the presidency of Lord Reay. The education of Indian women was the subject especially brought forward, as being at the root of all possible advance in their position. Lord Herschell mentioned the case of a widow of five years old [sic!?], who was now studying medicine under the help of the Association.	Westminster and Lambeth Gazette	21 Jun 1890
Royal Victoria Hall	On Tuesday Sep 9th, Professor J.B. Malden will give a lecture on the recent discoveries made by Stanley in 'Darkest Africa'.	Westminster and Lambeth Gazette	30 Aug 1890
Esher Street Congregation al Church, Kennington	Mr Kusel's lecture on ' Darkest Africa', incl. Stanley's Emil Pasha's Expedition.	Westminster and Lambeth Gazette	8 Nov 1890
Prince Duleep Singh at Westminster County Court	case of Houghton & Gun v. Prince Victor Duleep Singh, action to recover £16 for stationery supplied to the Prince in 1888. Warrant suspended for 'one week only' because the Prince was going to Paris, 'generally esteemed a rich man'.	Westminster and Lambeth Gazette	15 Nov 1890

Police News/ Westminster A troublesome Oriental	On Saturday a man dressed in the gorgeous costume of the Orientals, and calling himself Ooram Khan, was charged on remand with being disorderly outside Millbank. The unfortunate Eastern has it appears come to England to try and obtain a reversal of a decree by which in his own country, he has lost some property. He has been several times to the India Office, and was so persistent that he was locked up at Bow –Street Police Court. […] He was remanded to inquire further into his sanity.	Westminster and Lambeth Gazette	15 Nov 1890
The Oriental Once More	On Saturday the Oriental who has so frequently appeared before the magistrate was again brought up. Mr de Ruizen explained through an interpreter, that no papers could be given him with reference to his law suit, that if he would go back to India his passage should be paid	Westminster and Lambeth Gazette	29 Nov 1890
Mr Warren Trevor' Concert	mentions a Miss Ira Aldridge as the contralto singer, whose ' full tones were heard to advantage in a song by Mr Alfred Allen.	Westminster and Lambeth Gazette	13 Dec 1890
Miss Colenso and the Zulu Chiefs	Miss Colenso lectured on the Zulu question and ill treatment by British, on Feb 14th at the Working Men's College, Great Ormond Street. Comprehensive.	Westminster and Lambeth Gazette	21 Feb 1891
Kennington Liberal and Radical Association	There was a good attendance of the members of the Women's Liberal Association, and of the Kennington Liberal and Radical Association at the club rooms, 143, Upper Kennington Lane, to hear an address from Miss Colenso on 'Zululand and the Zulus'. Mr Naoroji (Lord Salisbury's famous 'Black Man') presided.	Westminster and Lambeth Gazette	21 Feb 1891
Lecture at Castle Lane, Westminster.	Mr Martin Wood entertained the youths of this well-known Institute by giving the story of Stanley's marvellous adventures in the Dark Continent, illustrated by fifty large lantern pictures.	Westminster and Lambeth Gazette	7 Mar 1891
Miss Colenso on England and Zululand	At a meeting of the Balloon Society on Friday in last week, Miss Colenso delivered an interesting lecture upon England's wrongs in Zululand. Comprehensive	Westminster and Lambeth Gazette	23 May 1891
Travelling 3, 500 Miles to see the Queen	Martha Ann Rix, a widow, was born into slavery in the US, bought by her father when she was a few years old and taken by him to Liberia, West Africa. She was one of 13 children, who were all sold into slavery and never met her brothers and sisters. She has been saving for fifty years, to make this journey. She made a quilt, white satin and coffee trees. Mr Alfred E. Jones, the head of Elder, Dempster & Co, agents for the steamer, is now endeavouring to get her an interview with the queen.	The Brixtonian	16 Jul 1892

The New Parliament	One paragraph on Mr Naoroji , 'the Indian gentleman who contested East Finsbury. Various questions concerning our rule in India are rapidly coming to the front, and they are likely to receive all the more attention with Lord Salisbury's "Black Man" in the British Parliament.' There seemed to have been some attempts of the press to influence the elections. They reported that he had received large sums of money from India. Mr Naoroji had to write them saying that this was unfortunately not true.	The Brixtonian	23 Jul 1892
Mrs Ricks, the Negress, at Windsor	76 year old lady (see above), was accompanied by Mrs. Robertson, the wife of an Ex-President of Liberia, and on arrival in England, Dr Blyden, the Liberian minister took action. Together with Mrs Blyden, her daughter, granddaughter, Mrs Ricks was received by the Queen. On Thursday, she had lunch with the Lord Mayor and Mayoress at the Mansion House.	The Brixtonian	23 Jul 1892
Zaeo in the County Court	Zaeo, of the Aquarium and Oxford Music Hall fame, was sued by the plaintiff, a young Indian to recover £20 for wages, alleged to be due to him, and money advanced. Verdict in her favour.	The Brixtonian	30 Jul 1892
Floral and Industrial Exhibitions at Stockwell	The Rev. H.P. Welshman, from the Melanesia Mission, lent many curiosities brought from the South Sea Islands. The Universities Mission to Central Africa, lent many relics, including musical instruments, and 'a slave yoke, on which blood marks were still visible', etc.	The Brixtonian	6 Aug 1892
No title	In discussing religious questions, Mrs Ricks, the African negress who recently visited the Queen, quaintly remarked:- "Man's religion shouldn't be worn like a cloak - all on de outside. It orter be mo' like a porous plaster. De world may not see it, but de man knows it's dar, an' his family knows it's dar, an' his family knows it's dar, an' a doin' of him good."	The Brixtonian	10 Sep 1892
No title	The Aquarium will soon have on show the new 'Siamese twins', only it happens that they hail not from Siam, but from Oressa, in India. Two 3 ½ year old girls.	The Brixtonian	10 Sep 1892
First Surrey Rifles	Some colonial conquest pieces were enacted at the regiment's garden fete	The Brixtonian	10 Sep 1892
The Liberian Negress	Back in Monrovia, Mrs Ricks sent a letter of thanks, which is printed in the paper.	The Brixtonian	24 Sep 1892
St Michaels Entertainment	At the end of article the next entertainment is described: a highly interesting dioramic exhibition, to be given by Mr T. Adkins. The subject is : "Africa: Egypt to Cape Colony".	The Brixtonian	10 Dec 1892

	Ida B. Wells, formerly editor if 'The Free Speech' on how the former manager of that periodical had lost an ear due to a wrongly attributed article on the lynching of Black men writes: 'How long must it be that the men and women of my race are outraged and murdered in this manner? The only ray of hope amidst this all this gloom is the knowledge that there is a little band across the water which will give it's time and energy to helping me keep before the world these atrocities, in the hope in time to reach the public conscience'.	Fraternity	July 1893
The Ethiopian Minstrels	With description of songs, etc. Seems to have been a group of young (white?) amateurs.	The Brixtonian	18 Feb 1893
Princess Jeje	The Zulu Princess Jeje is on a visit to England with her husband, a gentleman named Meek. They have been engaged for some time in mission work amongst the Zulus and, as might be expected, the power of the Princess for good in this direction has been considerable. Jeje is a remarkable woman in many ways, having great natural ability and force of character. She is closely connected with what used to be the Zulu Royal family, and is a cousin of Cetawayo.	Fraternity	Jan 1894
Sangahamo	Last month a Mandingo West African by the name of Umbetiquoa Sangahamo visited and delivered a brilliant lecture at Sunderland on 'The Manners and Customs of the Mandingoes'. The gentleman is a student at Durham University, and we hope that he will have a successful career, and become a useful man among his people.	Fraternity	Jan 1894
Prince Ademuyiwa	The meeting of the Court of Common Council on November 1 was attended by the West African prince Ademuyiwa, attired in a robe of many colours. In excellent English he acknowledged the courtesy of the Lord Mayor in inviting him to the meeting. A large amount of animated debate gave point to the prince's remarks which were heartily applauded both by the court and by strangers in the gallery.	Fraternity	Dec 1894
Local News	For stealing a rupee of the value of 2 shillings from a Lascar fireman in the Grapes Tavern in High Street Borough, Richard Stapple and William Hicks have been sentenced to 14 days hard labour from Southwark.	The Brixtonian	2 May 1896
The English in India	A most instructive and interesting lecture is to be delivered at the lecture room at 8 Mayall Rd, Brixton on the above subject by Mr. H. Heridas, a native of Bombay. As well as noting the good points of British rule, the speaker will show in 'plain, unvarnished statements the results of misrule' and will answer questions at the close.	The Brixtonian	4 July 1896
Local News	The Burmese workmen and women from the Crystal Palace paid a visit on Sunday to the Queen at Windsor and were seen by her Majesty in the Great Quadrangle of the castle. The party included silversmiths, wood-carvers, cigar makers, weavers and footballers. They were shown the State apartments and refreshments having been served they returned to Sydenham.	The Brixtonian	18 July 1896

Local News	The cricket batting of Mr. Ranjitsinjhi in first-class matches has resulted in 2757 runs thus beating the work of any batsman. Mr. WG Grace put together 2379 in 1871. The above is exclusive of the Indian's present scoring at Brighton.	The Brixtonian	5 Sep 1896
Editorial – Drink in India	Mr. H. Haridas from Bombay decries the levels of alcoholism in India, both amongst the 'natives' and the British.	The Brixtonian	24 Oct 1896
Brixton Independent Church	A lecture on the general history of Africa, incl. Egypt, and mostly focusing on South Africa by Mr. B.J. Malden, F.R.G.S., F.Z.S.	The Brixtonian	6 Feb 1897
South London and the Indian famine	List of donations to the Indian Famine Relief fund, see also subsequent issues for further entries.	The Brixtonian	13 Feb 1897
Camberwell Chips	Tonight (Friday) a prince of Mandigoland rejoicing I the name of Umbetiquasanghangamo will deliver what he calls a humorous and instructive lecture in Shawbury Hall in East Dulwich. The King of Benin and his people are to be described and the horrors and superstitions of African slavery duly depicted while the whole will be wound up with a vocal and instrumental concert.	The Brixtonian	13 May 1898
Thrashing a Black Boy	A young African by the name of Lioney was sent to Camberwell workhouse after being found running along the tracks and bleeding by the station master of Queen's Road Station. A Mr. Frank Bartlett was fined £5 for the offence.	The Brixtonian	13 May 1898
Lambeth Police News	A number of Algerians have been fined for hawking goods without a license.	The Brixtonian	24 Jun 1898
Lambeth Police News	An Algerian was charged 10 shillings and costs for selling goods without having a hawker's license.	The Brixtonian	1 July 1898
no title	Mr. J Dickerson delivered a lecture entitled 'My Life when a Slave' at the hall in Hindman's Rd. The chair was taken by Mr. Chandler the vice-president of the mission and the lecturer entertained his company with a stirring and interesting narrative of his life as a slave. He also sang John Brown's 'Emancipation' song…Mr. Dickerson has given this account of his slave life before the Queen and the Royal family.	The Brixtonian	9 Feb 1900
British Rule in India	Sir Mancherjee Bhownagree MP for Bethnal Green addressed the St. John's Literary and Debating Society. While generally praising British rule, he criticised Dadabhai Naoroji	The Brixtonian	25 May 1900

Appendix One

St Mary Lambeth Registers: Possible references to black people and foreigners 1670 - 1834

St Mary's Lambeth burials: John the son of Manby a stranger	11 Apr 1670	MRY1/P8 5/343
St Mary's Lambeth baptism: William the son of James Mar[?]umb Stranger	14 Jul 1670	MRY1/P8 5/343
St Mary's Lambeth burials: Theopholius the son of Theophilius Osee [?]	3 Oct 1670	MRY1/P8 5/343
St Mary's Lambeth baptism: Mary the daughter of Henry Nohito a stranger	25 Nov 1670	MRY1/P8 5/343
St Mary's Lambeth burials: Lanzano (?) Wakeman servant to Mr Garney (?)	25 Jan 1672	MRY1/P8 5/343
St Mary's Lambeth burials: Nicholas Proutingo (?) from the Marsh	5 May 1672	MRY1/P8 5/343
St Mary's Lambeth burials: Isabell a servant from Ffleere (?)	5 Jun 1672	MRY1/P8 5/343
St Mary's Lambeth burials: Obadia the Sonne of Obadia Serrynge (?)	3 Feb 1673	MRY1/P8 5/343
St Mary's Lambeth burials: Elizabeth a stranger from Peter Ollivares [Ollivers?]	13 Aug 1675	MRY1/P8 5/343
St Mary's Lambeth burials: Elizabeth the daughter of Walter Dehiree [Dohiroo?]	29 Sep 1675	MRY1/P8 5/343
St Mary's Lambeth burials: John the sonn of Mrs Mary Pendairusies [?] a stranger	23 Mar 1676	MRY1/P8 5/343
St Mary's Lambeth burials: Susannah the daughter of Wm Mopsey [gey?] a Str. and servant to [] Halford	21 Jun 1676	MRY1/P8 5/343
St Mary's Lambeth burials: Mary the daughter of Bathashazer Reading a Str.[86]	7 Jul 1676	MRY1/P8 5/343
St Mary's Lambeth burials: John the son of Thomas Terrah	3 Sep 1676	MRY1/P8 5/343

---

[86] entry for burial on same day: Joseph Reading a Parish child drowned. Both carry the same surname, were buried on the same day, but one is daughter of a Stranger and the other one a Parish Child?

St Mary's Lambeth burials: Elizabeth the daughter of James Gingo [ni?] a Str.	18 Dec 1676	MRY1/P8 5/343
St Mary's Lambeth burials: John Brindo a stranger	29 Dec 1676	MRY1/P8 5/343
St Mary's Lambeth baptism: Elizabeth daughter of [X]o[X]ozoo	7 Jan 1677	MRY1/P8 5/343
St Mary's Lambeth burials: John Sandsomo [e?]	8 Mar 1677	MRY1/P8 5/343
St Mary's Lambeth baptism: Elizabeth the Daughter of Goneiro [?]	1 April 1677	MRY1/P8 5/343
St Mary's Lambeth burials: Mary the Daughter of Henry	13 Jul 1678	MRY1/P8 5/343
St Mary's Lambeth burials: Alloda the wife of William Dokosiser	15 Sep 1678	MRY1/P8 5/343
St Mary's Lambeth burials: Joano [Joane?] a Servant to Mr Hoxcroft of Clapham	21 Oct 1678	MRY1/P8 5/343
St Mary's Lambeth burials: Mary the wife of Allexander Stranger.	4 Jan 1679	MRY1/P8 5/343
St Mary's Lambeth burials: George Lowo [Lewe?] a Stranger.	25 Jul 1679	MRY1/P8 5/343
St Mary's Lambeth baptism: Elizabeth the Daughter of Thomas Terra	20 Mar 1680	MRY1/P8 5/343
St Mary's Lambeth burials: Mary the daughter of Obadiah Fairclough	6 Aug 1680	MRY1/P8 5/343
St Mary's Lambeth burials: Joane Hobbo (s?) widow	7 Nov 1680	MRY1/P8 5/343
St Mary's Lambeth burials: Isabill the daughter of Luti Axum	26 Aug 1681	MRY1/P8 5/343
St Mary's Lambeth baptism: Edward the son of Satkuile Ride	9 Apr 1682	MRY1/P8 5/343
St Mary's Lambeth burials: Margaret the daughter of Milio Agar	16 Aug 1682	MRY1/P8 5/343
St Mary's Lambeth burials: Damiris (?) Kinte widdow	3 Aug 1683	MRY1/P8 5/343
St Mary's Lambeth baptism: Lying In Hospital Harriet Freeman/ William and Margaret/ Girl	25 Jan 1686	MRY1/P8 5/378[87]
St Mary's Lambeth baptism: Sarkuile son of Sarkuile Right	20 Feb 1686	MRY1/P8 5/343

St Mary's Lambeth burials: Andrew Lundikah (?): Stranger.	16 July 1687	MRY1/P8 5/343
St Mary's Lambeth burials: Sarah Stranger. [c cto Bas? some abreviation]	16 July 1687	MRY1/P8 5/343
St Mary's Lambeth baptism: William son of John Coshe	16 Oct 1687	MRY1/P8 5/343
St Mary's Lambeth burials: Elizabeth daughter of William Mak[n?]	20May 1694	MRY1/P8 5/343
St Mary's Lambeth burials: Ann the wife of Thomas Barefoot the Marsh	11 Jan 1698	MRY1/P8 5/343
St Mary's Lambeth burials: Elizabeth the daughter of John Bushman	3 Mar 1698	MRY1/P8 5/343
St Mary's Lambeth baptism: Elizabeth daughter of Thomas Batho South Lambeth	13 Nov 1698	MRY1/P8 5/343
St Mary's Lambeth baptism: Jonathan [gap in original] Whitchard aged about 13	19 Feb 1701	MRY1/P8 5/343
St Mary's Lambeth burials: Ann the daughter of widow moar? Kennington	11 Oct 1701	MRY1/P8 5/343
St Mary's Lambeth baptism: Susanna daughter of George Iron being [?] 5 years old	15 Jan 1702	MRY1/P8 5/343
St Mary's Lambeth burials: William the baseborn son of [gap in original] Coleback	13 Sep 1702	MRY1/P8 5/343
St Mary's Lambeth burials: James Gi[w? r?]odo Marsh	26 Dec 1702	MRY1/P8 5/343
St Mary's Lambeth baptism: Hannah Daughter of James Bell being about 18 years old [ye wale??]	21 Jun 1703	MRY1/P8 5/343
St Mary's Lambeth baptism: George son of George Iron about 9 years of age old i.d. [Vauxhall]	26 Mar 1705	MRY1/P8 5/343
St Mary's Lambeth baptism: Ann Daughter of John Bell [D?] 8 years of age	7 May 1708	MRY1/P8 5/343
St Mary's Lambeth baptism: James & George Freeman about 20 years of age	22 Jun 1712	MRY1/P8 5/343
St Mary's Lambeth baptism: Elizabeth the Daughter of John Duck [possibly Duke?]	15 Feb 1712	MRY1/P8 5/343
St Mary's Lambeth baptism: Martha the Daughter of James George Freeman	22 Jun 1712	MRY1/P8 5/343
St Mary's Lambeth baptism: George & James son of James Ogibre [?] Surgeon	25 Nov 1714	MRY1/P8 5/343

St Mary's Lambeth burials: Frances Fele	12 Feb 1716	MRY1/P8 5/343
St Mary's Lambeth burials: Benjamin son of Michael Freeman	9 May 1716	MRY1/P8 5/343
St Mary's Lambeth burials: Judith Daughter of Judith Oglevie [?]	3? Jul 1717	MRY1/P8 5/343
St Mary's Lambeth baptism: Adult baptism of James Dyson (parentage unkown)	5 Nov 1722	MRY1/P8 5/344
St Mary's Lambeth baptism: Elizabeth, daughter of William Home, baptised aged 13	25 Nov 1725	MRY1/P8 5/344
St Mary's Lambeth baptism: Samuel Houlton, adult and married	4 Apr 1728	MRY1/P8 5/344
St Mary's Lambeth baptism: Elizabeth, daughter of Plato	30 Apr 1729	MRY1/P8 5/344
St Mary's Lambeth baptism: Thomas Charles Pain	5 Sep 1738	MRY1/P8 5/344
St Mary's Lambeth baptism: Richard, son of Richard Morris and his wife Abigail	1 Apr 1739	MRY1/P8 5/344
St Mary's Lambeth baptism: Mary Davis baptised aged 35	26 Oct 1739	MRY1/P8 5/344
St Mary's Lambeth baptism: Ann Philby baptised aged 37	26 Oct 1739	MRY1/P8 5/344
St Mary's Lambeth baptism: Sarah Clark baptised aged 57	21 Nov 1740	MRY1/P8 5/344
St Mary's Lambeth burials: Edward Coco	8 Oct 1745	MRY1/P8 5/345
St Mary's Lambeth baptisms: John Lewis Son of John Blackmore and his wife Elizabeth	5 Feb 1758	MRY1/P8 5/345
St Mary's Lambeth burial: Robert Coco	24 Nov 1769	MRY1/P8 5/346
St Mary's Lambeth baptism: Ann Sherman, an adult aged 28 years	12May 1771	MRY1/P8 5/346
St Mary's Lambeth baptism: Kerenhappuch, daughter of John Whittaker and Mary	19 Apr 1777	MRY1/P8 5/347
St Mary's Lambeth baptism: Mauritius son of Mauritius Lowe and Elizabeth	19 Apr 1777	MRY1/P8 5/347
St Mary's Lambeth baptism: Emma Jane daughter of Arthur Owen by Frances Montresor, born at Madras in the East Indies aged 2 years	1 Dec 1777	MRY1/P8 5/347

Stockwell Chapel burial: Kerenhappuch Whittaker, Prince's Street	10 Nov 1778	MRY1/P8 5/347
Stockwell Chapel burial: William Barefoot	3 Dec 1779	MRY1/P8 5/347
St Mary's Lambeth baptism: Sarah Ann daughter of George Armstrong and Amilkia	28 Nov 1779	MRY1/P8 5/347
St Mary's Lambeth baptism: William son of Elizabeth Barefoot, baseborn	20 Dec 1779	MRY1/P8 5/347
St Mary's Lambeth baptism: Mary daughter of George Hemp and Elizabeth, born December 26 years	6 Dec 1780	MRY1/P8 5/347
St Mary's Lambeth baptism: Grace Obiah (Abiah?) daughter of John Hopwood and Grace Obiah	31 Dec 1780	MRY1/P8 5/347
St Mary's Lambeth baptism: William Blackmore son of Griffin Crane and Sarah	29 Apr 1781	MRY1/P8 5/347
St Mary's Lambeth baptism: Sarah daughter of Richard Blackman and Sarah	15 Jun 1781	MRY1/P8 5/347
Stockwell Chapel burial: Sarah Blackmoore, workhouse, poor	26 Aug 1784	MRY1/P8 5/347
St Mary's Lambeth baptism: Elizabeth daughter of William Blackman and Letitia	27 Feb 1785	MRY1/P8 5/347
St Mary's Lambeth baptism: Obadiah Anthony son of Alexander Thompson and Elizabeth	12 Oct 1785	MRY1/P8 5/347
St Mary's Lambeth baptism: Lying In Hospital James Freeman/ Francess/ Boy[88]	4 Dec 1797	MRY1/P8 5/378
St Mary's Lambeth baptism: Joshua Jaspe son of John Thompson and Karanhappuch	14 Jan 1798	MRY1/P8 5/349
St Mary's Lambeth baptism: Henry William son of William Odele and Mary	8 Jul 1798	MRY1/P8 5/349
Stockwell Chapel burial: Silvester Blackmore	3 Aug 1799	MRY1/P8 5/349
St Mary's Lambeth baptism: Lying In Hospital James Duke / Sarah/ Boy	17 Oct 1799	MRY1/P8 5/378
St Mary's Lambeth baptism: Robert son of Benjamin and Ann Blackmore	26 Dec 1800	MRY1/P8 5/349
Stockwell Chapel burial: Melchicidee Tipson, Union Row	10 Oct 1798	MRY1/P8 5/349

---

[88] The Lying in Hospital birth register had three entries besides the date: name of child/ parents name/boy or girl

St Mary's Lambeth baptism: Lying In Hospital Frederic Colliar/ Apsico/ Boy	10 Feb 1802	MRY1/P8 5/378
St Mary's Lambeth baptism: George Wilson born at Ceylon at East India in June 1778	10May 1802	MRY1/P8 5/349
St Mary's Lambeth baptism: Elizabeth daughter of William and Rebecca Blackmore	24 Oct 1802	MRY1/P8 5/349
St Mary's Lambeth baptism: Edward Hyncinth Bogle son of Edward Corbet and Marguerette Fatime Prin base-born at Jeremie in St. Domingo 31 Jan 1998	22 Aug 1803	MRY1/P8 5/349
Stockwell Chapel burial: Penelope Blackmore, Felix Street	21 Oct 1803	MRY1/P8 5/349
St Mary's Lambeth baptism: William Powell Nirdar son of John and Sarah Baxter born 8 Jan 1793	27 Nov 1803	MRY1/P8 5/349
St Mary's Lambeth baptism: Robert Powell son of John and Sarah Baxter born in 1796	27 Nov 1803	MRY1/P8 5/349
St Mary's Lambeth baptism: Lying In Hospital William Leopard/ Thomas and Elizabeth/ Boy	9 Aug 1804	MRY1/P8 5/378
St Mary's Lambeth baptism: George son of Obediah and Frances Blackman	14 Jul 1805	MRY1/P8 5/349
St Mary's Lambeth baptism: Lying In Hospital John Morah (?) / Jane/ Boy	1 Feb 1808	MRY1/P8 5/378
St Mary's Lambeth baptism: Lying In Hospital John Freeman/ Ann/ Boy	9 Feb 1808	MRY1/P8 5/378
Stockwell Chapel baptism: John William son of John and Susannah Proudfoot born 9 June 1806	29May 1808	MRY1/P8 5/379
Stockwell Chapel baptism: William son of John and Susannah Proudfoot born 8 May	29May 1808	MRY1/P8 5/379
St Mary's Lambeth baptism: Lying In Hospital Samuel Freeman / Frances/ Boy	27 Sep 1808	MRY1/P8 5/378
St Mary's Lambeth baptism: Lying In Hospital Frances Freeman/ Lucy/ Girl	19 Aug 1809	MRY1/P8 5/378
Stockwell Chapel baptism: Jonathan son of John and Susannah Proudfoot born 21 Jan	7 Apr 1811	MRY1/P8 5/379
St Mary's Lambeth baptism: James son of James Barton and Hagar Reed in Barbados 30 Nov 1804	9 Aug 1811	MRY/P85/ 349
St Mary's Lambeth baptism: Lying In Hospital Maria Blackmoar [more?/man?]/Thomas and Maria/girl [illegible abbreviation]	19 Dec 1812	MRY1/P8 5/378
St Mary's Lambeth baptism: Lying In Hospital Edward Sando/ Ann/ Boy	23 Sep 1815	MRY1/P8 5/378

St Mary's Lambeth baptism: Lying In Hospital Thomas Freeman/ Mary/ Boy	28 Apr 1816	MRY1/P8 5/378
St Mary's Lambeth baptism: Lying In Hospital Sarah/ Margaret/ Girl	22 Dec 1816	MRY1/P8 5/378
St Mary's Lambeth baptism: Lying In Hospital Matilda Freeman/ Sarah/ Girl	12 Aug 1818	MRY1/P8 5/378
St Mary's Lambeth baptism: Robert of Mary More/ Workhouse/ Soldier [89]	20 Aug 1820	MRY1/P8 5/352
St Mary's Lambeth baptism: Amuel James of Samuel & Elizabeth Hanam/ Brockstreet/ Clerk in Taxoffice	3 Sep 1820	MRY1/P8 5/352
St Mary's Lambeth baptism: Emily Sophia of Henry & Ann Freeman/ Burdett Street / Gardener	13 Sep 1820	MRY1/P8 5/352
St Mary's Lambeth baptism: William Israel of Thomas & Elizabeth Freeman/ Marsh/ Butcher	13 Sep 1820	MRY1/P8 5/352
Ann of Thomas & Elizabeth Freeman [T?]/ Marsh/ Butcher	13 Sep 1820	MRY1/P8 5/352
Caroline of Thomas & Elizabeth Freeman [T?]/ Marsh/ Butcher	13 Sep 1820	MRY1/P8 5/352
Charles Henry son of Charles & Mary Lepennell/ Felix Street/ Porter in the India House	9 Nov 1820	MRY1/P8 5/352
Sarah Ann daughter of George Harrison & Sara Bevil/ Townshend/ Clarindon & Vere [?] in Jamaica/ Propretor of Sugar Estates	23 Nov 1820	MRY1/P8 5/352
Frederick son of [parents' names gap] Ferrers [surname]/ Vine Street/ [gap occupation]	17 Dec 1820	MRY1/P8 5/352
Caroline China a foundling about a months old [Gaps]	21 Jan 1821	MRY1/P8 5/352
Charles son of Barzilla Ball & Martha Elizabeth/ High Street/ Carman	9 Feb 1821	MRY1/P8 5/352
Elizabeth daughter of Charles & Louisa Duffy/ Hooper Street [C?]/ Carver & Gilger	21 Feb 1821	MRY1/P8 5/352
Ethel (adult) daughter of Richard and Elizabeth Chalenor/ Somerstown/ Sailor	18 Mar 1821	MRY1/P8 5/352
St Mary's Lambeth baptism: Mary Daughter of Samuel & Sarah Laccohee / Vauxhall/ Cooper	22 Apr 1821	MRY1/P8 5/352
St Mary's Lambeth baptism: Richard son of William & Charlotte Matilda/ Gonarno [??] Oval/ Domestic Servant	23May 1821	MRY1/P8 5/352

[89] the register now includes: name of child/ parents' names/ surname/ abode/ occupation Was Mary More, the mother, a soldier?!

St Mary's Lambeth baptism: James Andrew of James and Sophia Fellagunn/ Marsh/ Domestic Servant	4 Jun 1821	MRY1/P8 5/352
St Mary's Lambeth baptism: Joseph son of Joseph & Fanny [Anny?] Cato/ Chapel Street/ Grocer	30 Jul 1821	MRY1/P8 5/352
St Mary's Lambeth baptism: Montgomery Walter son of Montgomery & Semiraimis [???] Williams/ Balmont Place/ Lietnt Royal Engineers	21 Aug 1821	MRY1/P8 5/352
St Mary's Lambeth baptism: Lying In Hospital Maria Hani/ Geraldmore & Elizabeth/ Girl	22 Sep 1821	MRY1/P8 5/378
St Mary's Lambeth baptism: Francis William son of Francis & Julia Addis/ Kennington/ Gardiner	17 Oct 1821	MRY1/P8 5/352
St Mary's Lambeth baptism: Charles Henry/ Jassuv de Carla & Mary Sowerby/ Meadplace/ Artist	23 Nov 1821	MRY1/P8 5/352
St Mary's Lambeth baptism: Mary Ann daughter of /Henry and Penelope/ Bonso/ Vauxhall/ Cheesemonger	19 Dec 1821	MRY1/P8 5/352
St Mary's Lambeth baptism: Freeman Duncan son of/ Lasco George + Harriet/ Dakin [Daku?]/ Stockwell/ Merchant	27 Feb 1822	MRY1/P8 5/352
St Mary's Lambeth baptism: Charles James (adult) son of/ Charles + Frances Cave/ Kennington Lane/ Welldigger	10 Apr 1822	MRY1/P8 5/352
St Mary's Lambeth baptism: John son of / John + Mary/ Blackman/ Kennington/ Taylor	28 Apr 1822	MRY1/P8 5/353
St Mary's Lambeth baptism: Harriet Caroline/ John + Mary/ Blackman/ Kennington/ Taylor	28 Apr 1822	MRY1/P8 5/353
St Mary's Lambeth baptism: Emma daughter of / Edward + Charlotte/ Tahourdia/ Oakley Street/ - - /	21May 1822	MRY1/P8 5/353
St Mary's Lambeth baptism: Edwin son of/ Mundee & Penelope/ Whitby/ Clayton Place/ Coal Merchant/	19 Jun 1822	MRY1/P8 5/353
St Mary's Lambeth baptism: Elizabeth/ Ralph & Elizabeth/ Kinkee/ Carlisle Place/ Musician	28 Jul 1822	MRY1/P8 5/353
St Mary's Lambeth baptism: Ellenor/ Ralph & Elizabeth/ Kinkee/ Carlisle Place/ Musician	28 Jul 1822	MRY1/P8 5/353
St Mary's Lambeth baptism: Elizabeth daughter of/ Francis + Ann/ Ennes/ Stangate/ Steward on Boat/ an Indiaman (deceased)	7Aug 1822	MRY1/P8 5/353
St Mary's Lambeth baptism: Jane daughter of/ Cotton & Maria/ Reeve/ Vauxhall/ Musician	16 Aug 1822	MRY1/P8 5/353
St Mary's Lambeth baptism: Stephen Berry Garner son of/ William + Rebeca/ Hadamstan/ Vauxhall/ Domestic Servant	30 Aug 1822	MRY1/P8 5/353
St Mary's Lambeth baptism: Elizabeth/ Ralph & Elizabeth/ Kinkee/ Carlisle Place/ Musician	28 Jul 1822	MRY1/P8 5/353

St Mary's Lambeth baptism: Sophie Mary/ George & Sophia/ Blakeman/ Marsh/ Steelpolisher	28 Oct 1822	MRY1/P8 5/353
St Mary's Lambeth baptism: Harbin James Richards son of/ James & Esther/ Elduton [Elderton?]/ Brixton/ Esq.	5 Nov 1822	MRY1/P8 5/353
St Mary's Lambeth baptism: William/ William & Monimia/ Congreve [?]/ Mason Str/ Gent	23 Nov 1822	MRY1/P8 5/353
St Mary's Lambeth baptism: Ann daughter oh Henry & Mary/ Blackman/ Heathfield Place/ Shoemaker	22 Dec 1822	MRY1/P8 5/353
St Mary's Lambeth baptism: Eliza/ Oliph Paine + Mary Street/ Workhouse/ Tailor	12 Jan 1823	MRY1/P8 5/353
St Mary's Lambeth baptism: Alice daughter of Eduard + Johanna/ Duke/ St Margaret's Westminster/ Butcher	18 Mar 1823	MRY1/P8 5/353
St Mary's Lambeth baptism: John son of/ Barnabas + Mary/ Richard [Rickard?] / South Lambeth/ Domestic Servant	19 Mar 1823	MRY1/P8 5/353
St Mary's Lambeth baptism: William/ Samuel + Sarah/ Laccohee/ Vauxhall/ Cooper	27 Mar 1823	MRY1/P8 5/353
St Mary's Lambeth baptism: James Wiliam/ Perry Dancer & Elizabeth Demnom […ni?]/ Nursey [Narsey?]/Luccas' Row/ Ship Broker	6 Apr 1823	MRY1/P8 5/353
St Mary's Lambeth baptism: Sidney the son of/ Elias Sycamore + Sarah Collins/ Workhouse/ Labourer	13 Apr 1823	MRY1/P8 5/353
St Mary's Lambeth baptism: George Frederic/ John + Jane/ Morland/ Hounslow/ Musician	16 Jul 1823	MRY1/P8 5/353
St Mary's Lambeth baptism: Eliza/ Oliph Paine + Mary Street/ Workhouse/ Tailor	12 Jan 1823	MRY1/P8 5/353
St Mary's Lambeth baptism: John son of/ John + Urela [v?]/ Emby/ Regent Street/ Carter	27 Sep 1823	MRY1/P8 5/353
St Mary's Lambeth baptism: Bethsheba daughter of / Richard + Ann/ Houghton/ Tower [?] Str St. Georges / Combmaker	28 Sep 1823	MRY1/P8 5/353
St Mary's Lambeth baptism: Thomas William son of/ John + Mary/ Duke/ Felix Street/ coachmaker deceased	28 Sep 1823	MRY1/P8 5/353
St Mary's Lambeth baptism: Cecilia (adult) daughter of John + Henrietta Matilda/ Pulley/ Elizabeth Place/ Artist (deceased)	19 Dec 1823	MRY1/P8 5/354
St Mary's Lambeth baptism: William Taylor son of/ Dymock [?] + Eleanor/ Shute/ Kennigton/ Shoemaker	7 Jan 1824	MRY1/P8 5/354
St Mary's Lambeth baptism: James son of John & Mary Sacoman [?]/ John Street/ Bootmaker	17 Oct 1824	MRY1/P8 5/354
St Mary's Lambeth baptism: John Samuel son of/ John & Clarissa Barbary [?] / Wood, St Ann's Westminster/ Servant	17 Nov 1824	MRY1/P8 5/354

St Mary's Lambeth baptism: Eliza Ann (adult)/ -- [parent's name] / Spencer/ Kennington/ Servant	24 Nov 1824	MRY1/P8 5/354
St Mary's Lambeth baptism: John Freeman son of / Edward & Sarah/ Lambert/ Park Street/ Labourer	26 Dec 1824	MRY1/P8 5/354
St Mary's Lambeth baptism: Sackville Samuel son of/ Sackvile & Elizabeth Hanam/ Caroline Street/ Shoemakers	22May 1825	MRY1/P8 5/355
St Mary's Lambeth baptism: Maria Sarah daughter of / John & Sarah Freeman/ Brock Street/ Tailor	20 Aug 1826	MRY1/P8 5/355
St Mary's Lambeth baptism: Alfred Hows [e?] son of / John & Sarah Freeman/ Brock Street/ Tailor	20 Aug 1826	MRY1/P8 5/355
St Mary's Lambeth baptism: Mary Ann daughter of / Samuel & Elizabeth/ Hanam/ Brok Street/ Clerk to Comissoners Kings taxes	1 Oct 1826	MRY1/P8 5/355
St Mary's Lambeth baptism: Hetty daughter of / John Lawton + Eleanor Haddan/ Paatt [?] Street/ Gent	13 Oct 1826	MRY1/P8 5/355
St Mary's Lambeth baptism: Augusta Elizabeth daughter of /Thomas Freeman & Catherine Elizabeth/ Mott/ South Vill[as?] [?]/ [ilegible, poss. Gent]	20 Oct 1826	MRY1/P8 5/355
St Mary's Lambeth baptism: Ambrose son of / Joseph & Catherine /Duke / Broad Stret/ Fisherman	3 Dec 1826	MRY1/P8 5/355
St Mary's Lambeth baptism: Eliza Ann daughter of / James & Mary/ Airzee [?]/ Princes Str./ Seaman	17 Dec 1826	MRY1/P8 5/355
St Mary's Lambeth baptism: Louisa and adult said to be 20 years of age/ Charles & Therese/ DeBlin/ Waterlo Road/ Officer in ye army (decd.)	24 Jan 1827	MRY1/P8 5/355
St Mary's Lambeth baptism: Jane daughter of/ John & Jane Bohag/ Richmond St./ Porter	12 Feb 1827	MRY1/P8 5/355
St Mary's Lambeth baptism: Margaretdaughter of Wiliam Andrew & margaret/ Roberts/ Chatto/ Brock [oo?] St./ Merchant Clerk	20 Jun 1827	MRY1/P8 5/356
St Mary's Lambeth baptism: Eliza duar of/ Robert & Mary / Blackmore/ Union St./ Carpenter	18 Jul 1827	MRY1/P8 5/356
St Mary's Lambeth baptism: Samuel son of/ Prudence/ Persona/ workhouse/ -- /	29 Jul 1827	MRY1/P8 5/356
St Mary's Lambeth baptism: Charlotte daughter of Benjamin Richard and Charlotte/ France/ Lambeth Walk/ painter [born in Mauritius/[90]	22 Sep 1827	MRY1/P8 5/356
St Mary's Lambeth baptism: Henry Soper [?] son of / James & Lydia/ Blackman/ Union Street/ Builder [?]	23 Sep 1827	MRY1/P8 5/356

---

[90] [note inserted:] Copy of a certificate of baptism from the register of the baptism in the protestant church of Port Louis in the island of Mauritus 14th May 1824 signed Edward Finch Civil Chaplain

St Mary's Lambeth baptism: Eliza daur of/ -- & - -/ Rush/ Norfolk Place/ Labourer	3 Sep 1828	MRY1/P8 5/356
St Mary's Lambeth baptism: Mary Ann Daughter of/ John & Mary/ Blackmore/ Regents Street/ Tailor	8 Oct 1828	MRY1/P8 5/356
St Mary's Lambeth baptism: John son of / -- / Hile [?]/ Smith St. / -- /	3 Sep 1828	MRY1/P8 5/356
St Mary's Lambeth baptism: Edward Freeman son of/ John & Elizabeth/ Linnington/ Cottage Place/ Cabinet Maker	3 Dec 1828	MRY1/P8 5/356
St Mary's Lambeth baptism: Elizabeth Daughter of/ Samuel & Sarah Lacoohee/ Vauxhall/ Cooper	12 Apr 1829	MRY1/P8 5/357
St Mary's Lambeth baptism: Norman son of/ Patrick & Mary/ Coucannou [?]/ Butts [?]/ Gardener	25 Oct 1829	MRY1/P8 5/357
St Mary's Lambeth baptism: Euphenica [?] daughter of John Nugent & Elizabeth Parks/ Barberie/ Walnuttree Walk/ Clerk in ye customs	2 Apr 1829	MRY1/P8 5/357
St Mary's Lambeth baptism: William Stewart son of Richard & Elizabeth [crossed out!] Mehetavell [?]/ Taylor/ The Island of Barbados/ Com [merc?]ial Officer	10 Sep 1829	MRY1/P8 5/357
St Mary's Lambeth baptism: Jane Lydia daughter of/ John & Mary Ann / Potto/ St George's Southwark/ Butcher	12 Sep 1830	MRY1/P8 5/357
St Mary's Lambeth baptism: Elizabeth daughter of Henry Hunter & Sarah Shillito/ J......A [?]/ Inn St./ Tinplate worker	10 Oct 1830	MRY1/P8 5/357
St Mary's Lambeth baptism: Sarah dau of/ Joseph & Rebecca/ Carou/ Gray's Walk/ out of business	22 Oct 1830	MRY1/P8 5/357
St Mary's Lambeth baptism: Henry son of/ Joseph & Sarah Mephibasheth [??]/ Gunnaway [a?]/ Pilgrim St./ Messenger in the council office	1 June 1831	MRY1/P8 5/357
St Mary's Lambeth baptism: William son of/ John Freeman & Mary Ann/ Potto/ Lambeth Walk Butcher	21Feb 1832[91]	MRY1/P8 5/358
St Mary's Lambeth baptism: (rec. into the church) Fanny daughter of/ John & Dorothy Duke/ Mead's Row/ Coachmaker dec.	26 Jul 1833	MRY1/P8 5/358
St Mary's Lambeth baptism: (rec. into the church) John son of/ Thomas & Mary Ann/ Duke/ Mead's Row/ Coachmaker dec.	26 Jul 1833	MRY1/P8 5/358
St Mary's Lambeth baptism: Mary Elizabeth daur of/ William Soper & Mary Babbacombe [?]/ Penhey [?]/ Vauxhall Row/ Oil Man	11 Aug 1833	MRY1/P8 5/358
St Mary's Lambeth baptism: Edmund son of/ John & Mary/ Blackmore/ Regent Street/ Tailor	20 Sep 1833	MRY1/P8 5/358
St Mary's Lambeth baptism: George Samuel son of/ John & Mary/ Blackmore/ Regent Street/ Tailor1833	20 Sep 1833	MRY1/P8 5/358

_____

St Mary's Lambeth baptism: Charles Frederick son of/ Frederick & Mary / Bonjour/ Waterloo Road/ Domestic Servant	22 Sep 1833	MRY1/P8 5/358
St Mary's Lambeth baptism: James Henry son of / William & Sarah/ Bantin/ Princes Road/ Bargeman	22 Dec 1833	MRY1/P8 5/358
St Mary's Lambeth baptism: Susanna daughter of/ George & Susanna/ Freeman/ Seville Place/ Compositor	14May 1834	MRY1/P8 5/358
St Mary's Lambeth baptism: Georgina daughter of/ George & Susanna/ Freeman/ Seville Place/ Compositor	14May 1834	MRY1/P8 5/358

Bibliography

The Black Prince, Cheap Repository for Moral and Religious Tracts. London [1795]

Clegg, Gillian, *Clapham Past,* Historical Publications, 1998

Cresswell, John, *Lambeth's Theatrical Heritage,* Streatham Society, 1991

Ducarel, Dr Andrew., *History and Antiquities of the Parish of Lambeth*, 1786

Engerman, Stanley, *Slavery,* Oxford University Press, 2001

Equiano, Olaudah, *The Life of Olaudah Equiano,* Longmans, 1989, ed. Paul Edwards

Fraser, Peter, *Before Windrush, The Early Black Presence in Hammersmith and Fulham,* Hammersmith and Fulham Archives, 2000

Fryer, Peter, *Staying Power: The History of Black People in Britain,* Pluto Press, 1984

Gibberd, Graham, *On Lambeth Marsh*, Jane Gibberd, 1992

Gerzina, Gretchen, *Black England, Life Before Emancipation*, Alison and Busby, 1999

Hennel, Michael, *John Venn and the Clapham Sect,* Lutterworth, 1958

Mayhew, Henry, *London Labour And The London Poor*, Enlarged Edition, London, 1861-2

Nicoll, Allardyce, *A History of English Drama*, 2nd Edition, Cambridge University Press, 1955-9

Oliver, Paul, *Black Music in Britain*, Open University Press, 1990

Prince, Mary, *The History of Mary Prince,* Penguin Books, 2000, ed. Sarah Salih

Rose, Lionel, *Rogues and Vagabonds: Vagrant Underworld in Britain,* Routledge, 1988

The Revels History of Drama in English; *Vol. VI, 1750 - 1780*, Methuen, 1975

Rydings, H A, *Prince Niambana in England* in <u>Sierra Leone Studies</u>, 1957

Sancho, Ignatius, *Letters of the Late Ignatius Sancho,* Penguin Books, 1995, ed. Vincent Carretta

Smith, Eric, *A Loyalist From Boston* in <u>Clapham Antiquarian Society Occasional Sheet</u>, no. 294, 1972

Smith , Eric, *Clapham Saints and Sinners,* The Clapham Press, 1987

Stedman, John Gabriel, *Narrative, of a five years' expedition, against the Revolted Negroes of Surinam, in Guiana*......... 1796

Thomas, Hugh, *The Slave Trade,* Picador, 1997

Tobin, James, *Cursory Remarks upon Mr. Ramsay's Essay*, London 1785

Walvin, James, *England, Slaves and Freedom, 1776 - 1838.,* Macmillan, 1986

Walvin, James, *Slavery and British Society, 1776 - 1846*, Macmillan, 1982

Sources

Chapter 1

LMA	MRY 1/P85/343 -50	St Mary, Lambeth: baptisms, burials, marriages (marriages to1797)	1669-1820
LMA	MRY 1/P85/352 - 357	St Mary, Lambeth: baptisms	1820-1834
LMA	MRY 1/P85/378	St Mary, Lambeth: Lying In Hospital baptisms	1794-1813
LMA	TR/145-6	Holy Trinity Clapham: baptisms, burials	1679-1833

Chapter 2

LAD	P1/2-7	St Mary, Lambeth: churchwardens accounts	1716-1850
LMA	LA/BG140/2-3	Lambeth: Rough Examinations	1837- 1839
LMA	P85MRY1/284	Account of Children born or taken into the workhouse	1771-1778
LMA	P85/MRY1/198-221	Settlement Examinations	1792-1834
LMA	P85/MRY1/231-8	Settlement Examinations, Westminster Lying In Hospital	1780 - 1816
LMA	H1GLI/B9-11	Settlement Examinations, Westminster Lying In Hospital	1812-1857

Chapter 3

LAD	12/951	Astleys Amphithetare collection	1820 - 1868
LAD	S5061	Bower Saloon collection	1846 - 1862
LAD	S5062	Surrey Theatre collection	1816 - 1870
LAD	IV/162/5-17	Vauxhall Gardens collection	1820 - 1854

Chapter 4

LAD	Westminster and Lambeth Gazette	Nov 1881-1891
LAD	Clapham Gazette and Local Advertiser	Nov 1853- Dec 1871
LAD	South London Press	De. 1865 - 1868
LAD	The Brixtonian	Jul 1892 - May 1900
BL	The Lambeth Argus, Vol 1	1840
BL	The South London Gazette vol 1	1855 - 1856
BL	South London Local Journal; subsequently South London Journal	1856 - 1859
BL	Fraternity	1893 - 1894

LAD: Lambeth Archives, **LMA**, London Metropolitan Archives, **BL**, British Newspaper Library